Earth Dreams

Finding Light in the Shadow

Elizabeth A. Brensinger

Red Road Press

First edition. First printing December 2001. Printed and bound in the United States of America; printed on 100% post-consumer, process-chlorine-free recycled paper with soy-based inks.

Grateful acknowledgement is made to the following for permission to reprint previously published and/or copyrighted material:

Ballantine Books, a division of Random House, Inc., for an excerpt from Paula Underwood's poem "Who Speaks for Wolf", published in *Intimate Nature: The Bond between Women and Animals* (Brenda Peterson, Deena Metzger, Linda Hogan, eds.), copyright © 1998

Broadway Books, a division of Random House, Inc., for an excerpt from *The Illuminated Rumi*, translated by Coleman Barks and Michael Green, copyright © 1997

HarperCollins Publishers, Inc., for excerpts from *Owning Your Own Shadow*, copyright © 1991 by Robert A. Johnson

Threshold Books, for two selections from *Open Secret: Versions of Rumi*, translated by John Moyne and Coleman Barks, copyright © 1984

Mark Kennedy, for lyrics from the CD "Sudama"

Jan Garrett, for lyrics from the CD "Don't Go Back to Sleep". www.jangarrett.com

Cover photo © Elizabeth A. Brensinger.

The following trademarks appear in this book: NordicTrack; Benadryl; Therm-a-Rest; Therma Lounger; Good Earth; Gore-Tex; Polysporin; Maglite.

ISBN 0-9713372-0-9

Library of Congress Control Number 2001119654

A portion of proceeds from the sale of *Earth Dreams* will be donated to organizations working to preserve the American wilderness.

* Note to organizations: Quantity discounts are available on bulk purchases of this book for educational or fund-raising purposes. For information, please contact:

Red Road Press
P.O. Box 71
New Tripoli, PA 18066
www.RedRoadPress.com

For the spirits of the canyons, and for all who listen for the Voice; may you find your own.

Acknowledgements

Woven into this book is the love and support of numerous beings -- many but not all of them two-legged -- whose contributions were critical to the realization of the dream that became *Earth Dreams*. And so, in no particular order, let me express my heartfelt gratitude to the following:

Karen Bashkirew, for helping me muster the courage to switch from third- to first-person, thereby putting myself where I belonged, in the midst of my own story.

Tracey Barry, whose enthusiasm for this project even in its earliest incarnation contributed greatly to mine. Tracey, I am so glad we were -- and are -- buddies; your generous heart and love for all beings is an inspiration.

Trebbe Johnson, for voicing excitement about *Earth Dreams* at a time when my own was fading, and for enriching the manuscript immeasurably with the suggestion that I put down "roots".

Linnea Johnson, who reminded me to stay in the canyons. Thanks for saving us all from aggravating detours.

Bill Plotkin, not only for sparing me an embarrassing blunder related to water purification but also, and far more significantly, for creating Animas Valley Institute, without whose work this book would not have been written and I would not be nearly as much myself.

Dorothy Mason and Betsy Levin for being my final "line of defense" -- the last readers of a nearly finished manuscript, whose suggestions and unabashed enthusiasm helped me remember what this project was really about and why I'd embarked on it when the nitty-gritty of self-publishing threatened to drown me.

Steven Foster for his generous support of me, a stranger, at a time in his life when time was especially precious.

Robert Johnson for the 4-leaf clovers -- I am certain that they helped!

Ann G.T. Young, whose support was gracious, unhesitating and essential.

Dave Heintzelman, who helped me see that converting this manuscript from Word to Quark without losing my mind was within the realm of possibility.

Susan Rubinstein, Mike Kline, Dianne Timberlake, Linda Glaeser, Autumn Van Ord, Becky Kear, Loraine Anderson, Chris Adams, JoAnne Jaeger, Lauren Chambliss, John Dunkle, Carol Adams, and Patti Rieser for forging their way through early versions of the manuscript, and for offering me encouragement nonetheless. Thanks too to all the other friends and acquaintances who periodically inquired about the project and otherwise showed they cared.

Janis Galitzeck and her colleagues at Alcom Printing for working with me to ensure that *Earth Dreams* would be printed in a manner that treads lightly on the Earth -- on 100% post-consumer, process-chlorine-free recycled paper with soy-based inks. Not only is it possible to do the right thing, and essential; it's becoming relatively easy!

My mother, Helen S. Brensinger, for introducing me to books at the earliest possible age, thereby instilling in me a lifelong love for the written word and giving me the gift that has become my work; and my father, the late Howard C. Brensinger, whose love for animals and our other non-human relations helped inspire my own.

Deer, Raven and the numerous other non-human

beings whose medicine has supported, challenged and nurtured me.

Tigger, who sat on my lap and kept me company during many a long day at the computer. I miss you every day, Tigger-boy.

Linda Hogan, Terry Tempest Williams and Jane Goodall for writing about the topics closest to my own heart, and for doing so passionately, eloquently and lovingly. Your lives and work are a gift to us all. And thanks to Barbara Kingsolver, a writer whose books have been both a joy and an inspiration to me; your courage in acknowledging complexity and speaking out for peace has shone especially bright in the post-September-11 darkness.

The Southern Utah Wilderness Alliance and other tireless activists dedicated to preserving the breathtaking, irreplaceable and utterly alive canyons I have come to love so deeply. As this book goes to print, the American wilderness is facing its most severe threat in years; the time to stand up in defense of wilderness -- and of our own souls -- is now.

Kenny Ausubel & Nina Simons for gifting the world with Bioneers, whose visionary & practical solutions for restoring the Earth bring hope, light and possibility to a world that desperately needs it -- and for throwing the most uplifting conference I've ever attended.

My 13 fellow questers and the guides and apprentices who shared in the October, 1997 AVI quest. I honor each of you.

Finally, I extend my deepest gratitude to Ann Adams, whose constant support of me and belief in my ability to rise to the occasion of my life were essential to completing this book. Ann, sharing this journey with you is a very great gift indeed.

"*We don't know where our gift will bear fruit, but we do know that our gift is required. .·. You are the light of the world. What permission are you waiting for before you feel as if you could offer your gift with ease and playfulness and grace? What is your gift to the family of the Earth?*"

-- Wayne Muller

Author's note:

Out of respect for the fragile desert ecosystem, I have chosen not to name the particular canyon where this story unfolded. Instead, I will simply call it The Canyon.

Introduction

> *"The teachings don't come like some people think. You can't just sit down and talk about the truth. It doesn't work that way. You have to live it and be part of it and you might get to know it. I say you might. And it's slow and gradual and it don't come easy."*
>
> -- Rolling Thunder, in the book of the same name by Doug Boyd

How the Earth Saved My Life. I typed the words and then sat staring at them, wondering what came next. Moments passed. I scratched the back of my hand, spun around a few times in my chair, looked expectantly at the computer screen as if some writer other than myself were about to resume typing. Nothing happened. OK, try again. *How the Earth and My Soul Conspired to Save My Life.* Everyone loves a great conspiracy theory -- particularly Hollywood! Perhaps this story, too, could eventually light up the screen? But who would play the conspirators? Not many actors clamoring to play the part of a raven, a sandstorm, or the shade cast cool by canyon walls. And besides, this conspiracy isn't sinister, it's loving. Would anyone care to read it? Would anyone dare to read it? *A Truth So Basic, Almost Everyone's Forgotten*

It. But since they've forgotten it for so long, how do I
know they'd be willing to remember? Sure, some part of
them wants to remember, is literally dying to remember!
But another part -- the part that earns them approval
and money and helps them feel safe, the part that curses
the status quo while adhering to it like paper to glue, the
part all-too-often mistaken for the whole -- that part will
fight to the death to stay cushioned and cozy in its
forgetfulness. *The Truth*. That's it, I thought. Simple, to
the point. *The Truth*. Like it or not, forget it or not, deny
it or not, it is the Truth. Turning away, satisfied I'd found
a possible title and already anticipating the taste and
feel of a steaming cup of Good Earth tea, I felt a smile
playing at the corners of my mouth. Ah-ha!, I thought.
Better still -- *The Truth I Learned from Shadow*. After
all, every writer likes to get some credit.

     Meanwhile, somewhere in a remote Utah canyon --
actually, at a very specific place in a canyon that, like
every one, is a canyon like no other -- the winter sun and
jagged sandstone walls cast a chilling shade over Lizard
Rock, juniper, prickly pear and sage. No human being
had been there since I'd left, nearly three months before,
so tired and so dirty and so inexplicably angry that I'd
barely glanced over my shoulder as our group hiked out
past the spot where I'd spent three days and nights
alone. Grit in my mouth, every step a conscious act of
balancing a 35-pound backpack against a nearly
incapacitating exhaustion and the ominous threat of a
fast-falling barometer, I told myself over and over again
that I could make it. "I'm young (2 months on the near-
side of 40; everything is relative; one of my fellow hikers
is SIXTY-THREE!), I'm strong, I can do this, I AM doing
this." Over and over again, until I -- and the guide who
pulled me up onto high rocks when my tired legs failed
me -- made it so. Until I shed my pack some two miles

10

hence, climbed into a car and settled in for the 150-mile wait for the showers -- the water I couldn't wait to feel streaming over and cleansing me. Sadly but not at all surprisingly, my inexplicable anger blinded me to the fact that, sand in every orifice notwithstanding, I was already the cleanest I'd been in years.

On the day that I faced my computer in the warmth and comfort of my East-coast home, it was a bone-chilling 29 degrees in The Canyon. Raven was there, circling the spot with audibly beating wings and a cry that blends honk, chuckle and froggish croak into a voice that careens forever off the walls of memory, evoking indelible images of sandstone and sky. Coyote, who'd laid low during the visit of the two-leggeds, loped along on a seemingly haphazard path, senses acutely tuned to the frequency of rabbits, mice and voles. The lizard who'd sat on the toe of my boot, watching me curiously as I watched lizard, had retired for the winter, hidden away from view. The cougar melted into the scenery, but then she always does that. And all the while, the Voice murmured quietly to any hearts that were open enough -- and near enough -- to hear.

I had heard the Voice during my sojourn in The Canyon -- sometimes clearly, sometimes as the stillness that waited on the far side of crazy jagged worrying, obsessing about nothing, my mind a hampster on a suspended wheel, scurrying wildly but going nowhere. Yet because its language was most often feelings, not words -- knowing, not thinking -- I found its story a hard one to write. More than anything, I realized, the Voice taught by experience and by example. It taught in symbols and in metaphor, using the natural world as its pen and pad. It taught by merging with the listener, becoming part of me in the same way that my bones and lungs and heart were part of me, breathing as I breathed, yearning as I yearned, laughing as I laughed, crying as I cried, and revealing as I sought. It taught by skillfully weaving its story into mine so that I barely noticed the extra pages unfolding. Unlike humans, their words and their actions so often inconsistent, the Voice was steady and unflinchingly honest. The Voice simply Was. If only telling its story were half that simple, I mused. "Begin at the beginning." Fine advice when the beginning is clear. The fact is, the Truth. Just. Is. No beginning, and certainly no end. So let me begin this telling in the same way that I began my journey to The Canyon -- with a leap of faith.

Chapter 1

*"I'm just trying to wake up -- I'm so afraid of
sleeping all my life and then dying -- I want to
wake up first! I wouldn't care if it was just for
an hour, as long as I was properly alive and
awake."*

-- Philip Pullman, *The Amber Spyglass*

I traveled to Utah's southeastern canyonlands to
enact a vision quest, described in the brochure as "a
ceremonial descent into the mysteries of the soul, serving
to uncover and retrieve the deepest passions and wisdom
of the heart, and the essence of each individual's life
purpose."

Vision quest. A term European anthropologists had
devised to describe a sacred dreaming journey known to
all great spiritual traditions -- a journey in which a
human being ventures alone into the wilderness to seek
clarity and direction and spiritual connection. A "journey," three days and nights spent nearly motionless -- the
body still, the heart open, listening for the Soul's Voice,
for the Voice of Great Spirit.

Vision quest. In North America, the Lakota term

to describe this journey into the known-unknown translates roughly as "lamenting." Expressing grief to gain vision, letting tears wash away the veil between the worlds. A classic lament, phrased in modern language? "I'm at the end of my rope," said our guide, "and my people are dying" -- people meaning everyone and everything important to you, Homo sapiens or not. "Imagine our brochures," he quipped. "Lamenting. Come to Utah to lament." Not exactly "See the USA in a Chevrolet" now, is it? What would an advertising firm do with that one?

When I'd boarded the plane for southwestern Colorado, first stop on the road to The Canyon, I hadn't heard of the Lakota translation. Had I been asked, though, I could have listed the fuel for my own lament: Painful decades-old memories, only recently recalled and throbbing like a sand-scraped knee, cleansed raw by salt-water, the feelings of pain and betrayal they stimulated stuffed so deep that they'd trapped other feelings beneath them -- feelings of joy and aliveness, to name but two. The fact that, all around me, I saw the world being torn apart -- figuratively in some cases, literally in others, seemingly irrevocably, in almost all. The fact that I was nearing 40 and still unclear about how best to live my life. The fact that I had been working on a book for 2½ years, yet couldn't seem to finish it.

Fuel for a formidable lament, yes. But as motivators for doing a vision quest, all of these paled in comparison to one: I simply had no choice.

Ever since childhood, I'd felt a close connection to nature and retreated there for rejuvenation and renewal. Ever since college, give or take a few lost years, I'd consciously been on a spiritual journey. So when I first read about vision quests -- spirituality in the heart of nature -- I was naturally interested. I was curious. I was excited. I was terrified. And if the truth be told, I doubted I'd ever do one. And so it was that every year I looked through the Omega Institute catalog, pausing at the page describing vision quests, mentally noting "ahh, a vision quest. I really should do one sometime!", then turning the page and eventually settling on some stimulating yet safe workshop at a retreat center where I'd know what to expect and what would be expected of me. And I wouldn't think about vision questing again until the next year, when I'd open the Omega catalog, pause at the page describing vision quests, mentally note "ahh! a vision quest. I really should do one sometime!", turn the page, and ultimately choose a Caribbean retreat. And so the cycle continued, unchanged. Until the year I opened the catalog to the page listing vision quests and knew, with the kind of knowing that defies doubt or explanation, resistance or rationalization, that this was the year I would go on a quest. Catalog closed.

It was the year I had no choice, because it was the year I hit bottom -- maybe not The bottom, but certainly the lowest low to which I'd sunk to date. Wrestling with the aforementioned fuel for my lament, I'd been pinned to the mat. Lost my perspective. Lost my sense of humor. Lost the ability to bounce back, let alone to move forward. Lost the free flow of my own emotions. Except for rare instances, lost hope. And most of all, lost the vitality for living. True, most people had no idea that I was anything other than the competent, relatively functional person I'd always appeared to be. No matter; I knew the truth even if they didn't. As I told my fellow questers between choking sobs during our first meeting together, my inability to live fully had become intolerable to me.

And so I'd had no choice but to do a vision quest; in order to really, fully, truly live, extreme measures were

15

called for. I needed something to blast me out of the hole (a.k.a. depression) into which I'd sunk. Carrying a way-too-heavy backpack for several miles over rugged terrain in order to spend three days and nights alone and fasting in the wilderness seemed to fill that bill, quite nicely.

Which didn't mean I wasn't scared. So scared, in fact, that in the weeks before my departure I crashed my knee into the handle of a wheel barrow, slammed my foot full-force into a log while playing wildly with my dog one night, tripped up the stairs and injured a toe. I caught a cold, developed ulcers in my mouth, suffered a sore throat. But despite my subconscious' best-worst efforts at sabotage, no bones were broken and no illness was debilitating enough to justify my staying home.

Chapter 2

> "Each child, each fledging hero, must walk the
> path, battle the dragons, and find the grail in his
> or her own way."
>
> -- Trebbe Johnson, "The Monster of Grim
> Prospects"

So it was that I came to be standing atop a
remote mesa in southeastern Utah, peering down into a
canyon -- the first canyon I'd had the privilege of visiting,
a canyon that took my breath away in a vast region of
sky and rock and awe-inspiring vistas that felt like home
despite looking nothing at all like it. I shifted uncomfort-
ably beneath the weight of my pack, peering down into
the shadows and creases and cracked-wide-open spaces
of this canyon that had somehow called me, reaching
across hundreds of miles to pluck me like a fruit, ripe for
this journey into self, into wilderness, into wilderness of
self. And as I looked, squinting into the sun, I did what
our guide suggested -- I imagined that my soul was
waiting for me down there amongst the sandstone and
the sage. Soul, that part of myself that knew why I'd
come to Earth, and what I came to do here. Soul, my own
unique manifestation of the universal Spirit. Soul, whose
view is more expansive, even, than this one. Soul, the
deepest richest essence of me. Imagine, he said, that you

and your Soul agreed to meet here in this canyon. I did,
and my eyes brimmed over with grateful tears.

I went to the canyons because I had no choice. And
perhaps I had no choice because this was the time -- the
time my soul had picked to save me.

Which still didn't mean that I wasn't scared. So
scared, in fact, that I had to deny any fear at all as we
began our descent into the canyon, a single-file line of
hikers snaking its way slowly along sandstone walls,
past sharp drop-offs, ever-deeper into the arms of the
Earth. I had to deny my fear because otherwise I might
have crumbled to my knees or stumbled over the edge or
simply stopped walking, my fear an obstinate ass
unwilling to go further. And if I hadn't been able to go on
there, how would I have been able to go on anywhere? So
I walked, focusing virtually all my attention on the
placement of my feet, grateful for breaks in which we
removed bulky packs and gulped water greedily -- but
not too greedily, lest we run out before reaching base
camp and a chance to pump and filter our next few
quarts.

An hour or so later we reached the canyon floor,
turned and hiked west -- west, the direction of the setting sun, of falling darkness, of introspection; the
direction, some would say, of the vision quest itself -- our
journey flatter now but no less long. For much of it, we
hiked through thick undergrowth that became over-
growth as it stretched sometimes above my head,
clutching at bare legs and leaving behind trails of itchy
red welts and feelings rubbed more raw than skin.
Unlike our guides, I had no frame of reference to know
that when we finally emerged from this errant jungle --
we were in a desert, for god's sake! -- base camp was just
a 20-minute stroll away. And because I didn't know,
because I couldn't see the end of the journey, I felt

fatigue crushing me like a giant's thumb.

Fortunately, though, my not-knowing interfered not in the least with our arrival at the place where we would camp together for 2½ days, preparing further for our three days and nights alone: base camp. To the unpracticed eye -- mine -- it looked scarcely different from other places we'd passed, except for a giant cottonwood tree whose branches virtually begged to be sat beneath. But to the guides it offered the all-important if less-obvious attributes of a good campsite -- several spots that were relatively flat and surrounded by trees or rocks or straggly bushes, making them suitable sites for erecting tarpaulin shelters; and, of course, water. Our camp was adjacent to a running creek that had been our companion -- albeit an often-invisible one, its presence evident only in cracked clay and displaced vegetation -- for most of our hike along the canyon floor. Here, however, water emerged from the underworld to flow freely. Behind us, red rocks reached up in jagged king-sized steps to the mesa-top; across the creek -- an easy walk over the exposed sides of partially submerged rocks -- they did the same. We were in the bottom of a massive "V", cradled by the Earth, our thirsts about to be quenched.

Still, I was exhausted. A fellow quester broke into a joyful run -- her pack, amazingly, still on her back, her stamina exceeding mine by at least the length of Utah -- and I felt like throttling her. Instead, I joined her and two others in setting up a tarp, putting down ground cloths, unrolling sleeping pads and bags and otherwise making camp. "*Once here*," I wrote later in my journal, "*I fell into my inept mode. Was very little help with the tarp* (knot-tying never a strong suit). *Contaminated my water filter on the first try, lost a contact lens. What the hell am I doing here?*"

Chapter 3

What I was doing there, according to a letter I'd written the day before, was waiting to be (re)born. That letter had been just one of many steps in tilling the field of feeling, the soil in which our dreams would grow, but for me it had been an especially big one. Asked to write a letter to the person least likely to understand my decision to quest, I'd chosen instead to write to a child -- not any child, but The child, The child I'd never borne and, at nearly 40, almost certainly never would. *"I ask your forgiveness for not bringing you into the world"* I'd written, *"though I feel certain it is I more than you who has suffered.*

"In this life," the letter continued, *"it has been me whom I've needed to birth. I am on this quest to fully give birth -- to me."*

Some pages later, after a circuitous journey not unlike its writer's, the letter ended where it had begun, with the theme of giving birth. *"If I tell the full truth,"* I'd written, *"I must admit that it was fear that first dissuaded me."* Fear. Fear had been one of the many variables

20

that had led me to face my 40s, childless. Would fear keep me from giving birth to myself, as well? If I were to successfully midwife my own rebirth in the womb that is The Canyon, I'd have to do so in the shadow of Fear.

The very next evening, our first evening in The Canyon, fear sat down quietly beside me in the circle beneath the cottonwood tree where we gathered to eat and talk. I assembled my Therma Lounger camp chair for the first time and collapsed into it, staring at the campfire and feeling detached from the joking and laughter and levity that pervaded this flickering oasis in the desert night.

It was at least the third time I'd felt this way -- in the midst of the group, yet very much alone -- since the 19 of us had met three very long days before. One of those times had been the night of the sweat lodge, watching the building of the fire that would cook the rocks that would produce the steam that would "cook" all of us, producing rivers of sweat to quench the thirst of the Earth -- She who soon would quench our own. That night, two nights ago, I'd sat there, my loneliness pressing me down down down toward the center of the Earth. "*The pit in my gut, again,*" I wrote. "*I know it has something to teach me . . .an old friend, really. Perhaps it has to do with being among people, yet feeling apart. Feeling alone. Feeling sad. Ah! Perhaps the feelings -- the sadness -- that I stuffed came to reside in my gut -- a heavy weight, so heavy that they've created negative pressure, a 'black hole' deep inside. Perhaps as I identify and release my feelings, the pit will disappear, filled up with all the parts of myself that fled, filled up with my authentic self.*"

Shortly thereafter, during the hours in which the fire raged and the rocks began to glow, we held a fear council. Going around the circle, one by one, as many times as it took (and it took many!), we each gave voice

to the things that we most feared -- the monsters that we
were afraid would ambush us in the canyons, eating us
for dinner or exposing us as frauds. In fact, virtually all
the fears fit into one of these two categories: the fraud
category, which held that nothing would happen on the
quest, proving us unworthy or unskilled or terribly
unconnected; and the eaten-for-dinner category, which
contained seemingly endless variations of bad things that
could happen, from getting sick to going crazy to being
attacked by a cougar. For me the greatest fear was also
of attack, but not by a wild animal. I was afraid of being
attacked by a human. When I voiced that fear, murmurs
of agreement reached out to me from all around the circle
-- not just from the women, it turned out, but also from
several men. And suddenly I ceased feeling alone in the
group. Fear -- usually the thing that builds walls
between us, as it did on the night of the campfire in The
Canyon -- in this case tore them down. We were all
human; we wanted the same things; we feared many of
the same things too.

Yet now that we'd arrived in this remote canyon,
attack by a crazed lunatic couldn't have seemed a more
remote possibility.

And so, my fears during the next two days were
much more subtle, adopting the guise of simple worry:
Would mold grow on my water filter in just one night,
since I'd forgotten to leave the bag unsealed and now, in
the midst of darkness, didn't know if I could retrieve it
from my pack without disturbing my sleeping tarpmates?
Was that slow burn in my abdomen the sign of an
approaching illness? What if I dug my "cat holes"
incorrectly? (To the uninitiated reader: Envision the most
beautiful "litter box" in the world.) And finally -- and far
more seriously -- what if I couldn't find my power spot?
Well, what if I couldn't?!?

Chapter 4

A "power spot" is that place on the Earth where
one goes alone to cry for a vision. In traditional
indigenous cultures, an elder or shaman often assigned a
power spot to a person preparing to enact a vision fast.
In modern western culture, in the new-old blend of traditions in which I quested, the quester finds his or her own
solo spot -- or, ideally, the spot finds her. Choosing a
power spot, in other words, isn't about using the rational
mind. Sure, there are practical matters to consider --
questing in a creekbed, for instance, no matter how
parched the ground beneath you, is a really poor idea;
rain so far up-canyon that the sky above you never
clouds can send a torrent of rushing water fierce enough

to drown you. Questing under an overhang streaked by dark lines isn't such a great idea, either. They tell anyone who'll listen of the passage of flowing water; if it rains, someone crouching underneath will most certainly get wet. In fact, there are a surprising number of places one can get wet -- really wet -- in a desert canyon. The canyons are full of washes -- paths that rushing water takes on its center-ward journey, which during dry weather are delineated by their form (subtly trough-like), the absence of vegetation, or a concentration of small rocks and gravel. During a rainstorm, these washes become the shimmering gushing roaring channels that connect waterfalls cascading gloriously from mesa-top to canyon floor. But most of the time, they lie sleeping, and it's incumbent on the backpacker to watch out for them.

On the day that we went out in search of our solo spots, however, the rational part of the mind that watches for creekbeds and dry washes could relax. We set out under dark clouds and soon found ourselves in a deluge -- rain that stung like tiny chunks of buckshot, diving in sheets that were thick enough to blind us. At the start of the heaviest rain -- a storm that turned on every "faucet", awakened every wash, tripled the width of the creek in minutes -- my buddy and I scrambled over boulders into a cave the size of a closet, where we crouched down beneath the thunder that ricocheted off sandstone walls. Inside, we were spiders, we were mice, we were lizards; it was 100 years earlier and 100 years hence. The air in that cave was so still that the stories of centuries could rest there -- and in those stories, human beings were just two words. Perhaps it had been 1,000 years, not one, since the last two-legged had been there; perhaps an Anasazi man or woman -- ancestor of Hopi and Pueblo -- had, like us, huddled inside, waiting out the rain. Or then again, perhaps no human had ever

been there. It was a possibility, and it made me a wolf
and a coyote and a cougar. It made me wild. And so we
waited there, crouched on all fours, until the rain slowed
and the thunder was just a far-off echo. Then, pulling
centuries on with our raingear, we set out on two legs to
resume the aborted search for our power spots.

    We were, once again, just vision quest buddies; as
such, we would be checking on each other once a day
during our three-day, three-night solos. We'd do so not by
visiting each other's sacred place -- because then, after
all, the solo would be less a solo -- but rather by building
a stone pile halfway between. Tracey would leave a stone
in the morning; I'd leave one in the afternoon; and if
either of us failed to do so, the other would commence a
search. That meant we had to know where each other's
power spot was -- and, unless we wanted to hike long dis-
tances on empty stomachs and still-emptier heads to visit
the stone pile, we'd have to choose spots in the same
general area of The Canyon.

    And so the two of us wandered together, trying to
do so aimlessly, trying to let ourselves be called. We
climbed up ridges, followed deer trails, peered behind
gnarled pinyon pines and humpbacked, lichen-specked
rocks. Where there was cryptobiotic soil, we stepped
gingerly. "Crypto": Resembling hundreds of miniature
drip castles made from the blackest sand, it is life at its
most brittle, a living soil composed of algae, lichen, moss
and bacteria on which plant life in the desert utterly
depends. Cryptogamic soils take 10 or more years to
mature, and a mind-boggling 50-250 years to recover
from being trampled. Literally, then, one careless step
can set life in the canyons back more than 100 years. So
we watched out for crypto as we walked, trying to feel
the pull of those sacred places that already lived inside
us but were manifested here on the physical plane,

somewhere in The Canyon.

Somewhere, for sure . . . but where?! After what
seemed like a long time of climbing and hiking and fruit-
less searching, my buddy found a spot that she liked. It
was back a side-canyon, and despite the vastness around
us and the light cold rain that continued to fall, this
place somehow felt safe and cozy. Like a warmly lit cabin
window peering out into chilly night, it beckoned. So
Tracey had succeeded where I, so far, had not; she'd
found a place that called to her. As for me, I began to feel
an even greater pressure to find my own place, urgency a
nervous quickening inside that threatened to cross the
line into irritability or, worse yet, an impulse to pick any
old spot at all.

Instead, I tried to open further the ears of my
heart, to feel the pull of a place, not reach out and grab
one. I thought back to a visualization from the day
before, in which I'd called upon guides -- spirit, not literal
-- for help in locating my power spot. With their assis-
tance, I'd relaxed onto a large flat rock in my imagination, warmed not just by the sun above but also by the
solar-heated surface of the rock below. I'd felt
inexpressibly, undeniably, gloriously loved and safe in
that warm and sunlit space; and sometime during my
rest there I was given this message: my power spot
would be somewhere I could fly to. Being human, not
bird or raptor, I assumed that meant my spot would be
elevated above the canyon floor and that an easy walk
would get me there.

And sure enough, I found it -- or rather, it found
me. Not more than 10 minutes from Tracey's spot, hiking
along a deer trail through wet and scratchy canyon
grasses, we came upon two flat rocks reminiscent of the
one in my waking dream. The first was large enough to
lie on, though its slope and position would make climbing

onto it a challenge; the other looked vaguely like a lizard's head and rose up at a 45-degree angle, creating a sheltered space just large enough to comfortably lean back in. That place under Lizard Rock pulled me; my body yearned to lie down on its miraculously dry sand floor. Instead, I walked 15 steps further in the faster falling rain to check out a mostly sandy, mostly flat area large enough to spread out on, surrounded by just enough scrubby-looking desert plants to approximate a tarp site. There was prickly pear cactus, too, but not too much to avoid sitting or stepping on. Looking up, I met the steady gaze of a juniper tree, gaunt and wild-looking, strangely beautiful; overlooking juniper stood giant red-rock beings, one resembling an eagle, and another, a pre-Colombian deity far from its home in some verdant Mayan jungle. Despite or perhaps because of the rain, the scent of sage was so thick it was almost palpable. As promised in my vision, this spot was indeed elevated above the canyon floor; it offered a wonderfully expansive view and was backed by more rocks and ridges higher still, reaching up eventually to the mesa. And getting there certainly had been easy. I looked down and saw deer scat, looked cross-canyon and imagined the morning sun peeking over craggy rocks to awaken me. This was it, search suspended.

Only then did I walk over to Lizard Rock, bend down and place on the sandy ground a small lapis point that I'd carried in my pocket for years. Lizard Rock, allow me to introduce myself. My name is Liz; this is my energy; tomorrow I'll be back.

Chapter 5

> *"Fear is not to be avoided, repressed, or conquered. For from the very depths of fear itself arises fearlessness, awareness, and wisdom."*
>
> -- Laura Simms, "Through the Story's Terror"

It wasn't until we returned to base camp that I realized I'd left more than a lapis point somewhere down in that rain-drenched canyon. Searching my backpack, my pouch, my pockets, I realized with a pang of sadness that I couldn't find my feather. It was a grouse feather, and it had come to me on the Appalachian Trail back home, waiting quietly, as all feathers do, until I'd glanced down and seen it lying by the toe of my boot, its bold lines barely visible beneath a shroud of dust. That grouse feather symbolized many things to me, not least of all the quest itself. I'd found it during a hike to break in my hiking boots; it had felt like a gift from the Creator, a positive sign, an affirmation of my intention to enact a quest. Later I'd read that the Plains Indians dance a spiral dance to honor grouse, and that Native Americans often painted the spiral, an ancient symbol of birth and rebirth, on their bodies prior to a vision quest to enhance their chances of receiving a vision. And so I'd brought Feather with me to the canyon -- a kindred spirit, perhaps, or at the very least a comfort. And now Feather was gone.

I didn't grieve long, however. The moment of sadness at the loss of Feather was fast overtaken by another moment in which I discovered that my sleeping bag had gotten wet, which triggered a series of other moments in which I first panicked -- how could a wet sleeping bag possibly keep me warm on cold canyon nights? -- then eased into worry, which was dispelled only an hour of moments later when the sun came out and I was able to join my fellow questers in hanging our soaked belongings on rapidly drying rocks. Later, I sat atop a large rock facing the churning, muddy creek that no one could cross, watching clouds roll by. "*Hopefully, no more rain,*" I wrote in my journal. "*The weather changes so quickly here; no sooner did I 'strip down' to shorts and turtleneck, than I had to put on the layers again. Even now I'm rather cold. My moods here change quickly, too. So does the degree to which I'm fully present, and the degree to which ego plays all its old tricks on me.*"

Obviously, a lot of those old tricks had to do with worry and with fear. Fear had grown way too big in my life; even though I knew, absolutely knew, how destructive Fear was, still I couldn't shake free. Fear clung to me, restricting my movements, constricting my heart. On some level I must have known all along that a major reason for coming on the quest was to face my Fear. My soul knew what I needed; the next day, I got my first dose of powerful medicine.

Chapter 6

"The understanding that I could die on the salt flats is no great epiphany. I could die anywhere. It's just that in the foresaken corners . . . there is no illusion of being safe."

-- Terry Tempest Williams, *Refuge: An Unnatural History of Family and Place*

It's mid-day on the first day of my solo. Several hours ago I walked away from our severance ceremony, not looking back because I didn't have to, knowing that the love of 18 people trailed along behind. I hiked for 15 minutes or so, dragged myself up the short but steep slope to my power spot, my feet struggling to maintain forward momentum on loose and slipping sand, and immediately pricked a finger on a thorn bush. That's how I introduced myself to this place a second time -- through giving the land a taste of me. Later I cut my thumb while carving excess wax from the wick of my candle lantern, drawing blood again. Seems clear that I'll have to bleed emotionally on this quest. Now, though, I have a more immediate concern: I've contaminated my water filter, already. Dropped the output tube into a puddle of

30

crystal-clear rainwater (ah! but appearances can be deceiving) captured in the crevice of a sandstone slab. To find it, I had to walk through quicksand. That's because the creek at The Canyon's heart is "running red" -- roiled by yesterday's rainstorms, it's water as nearly solid as any liquid can be, water so dense it seems about to rise up, take shape and run down the canyon on four swift legs. It's silt-rich water, palpable proof of how the canyons came to be; dangerous water that would clog my filter almost instantly, rendering it useless. So, it's rain-water puddles I had to seek, and a narrow side canyon I followed to get here.

Now I root through my backpack and pull out my journal, safe from moisture in a plastic ziplock bag. Remove the journal; fill the bag with precious, filtered water from the almost-empty 2-gallon container -- now emptier still -- that I've brought with me, hoping to fill; drop in a few iodine tablets; and submerge the output tube to cleanse it. I'll have to wait 15 minutes, then start all over again, pumping and filtering water from the puddle. But the bag leaks. Agonizingly slow drops. Will there be any water left at the end of 15 minutes? Will there be enough water for the iodine to purify the might-be-contaminated tube? If not, what then? I brought only a few iodine tablets with me -- and those, only because Wendy, a fellow quester, practically forced them on me. Thank god she did. But I definitely don't have enough tablets to purify three days' worth of water; I need this filter. I sit down on a rock, attempt to plug the holes with my fingers, and wait. Five minutes pass, then seven, eight. It's too early for me to sit, unmoving, for 15 min-utes; I'm still too agitated, hyped up. The fatigue of fast-ing is still a stranger; today is only day two of four long days sans food, and my early-morning nausea is barely a memory. I get up, taking care to keep my fingers over the

holes in the plastic bag, walk a few steps back toward
the main canyon and then cut off to the left, up a narrow
wash. Suddenly, I hear it. A strange sound, here. A
human-made sound, without question. Machine-like.
Relentless. Droning. Obviously, something mechanical
making its way down the main canyon. Moving where it
doesn't belong. Noisy. Crude. Caring about nothing: Not
about crushing the precious cryptobiotic soil that sustains plant life in the desert; not about me, a woman
alone and vulnerable in the wilderness. Just around the
bend, I feel this creature's hot mechanical breath, and it
tastes like panic. The collective unconscious and my own
life experience weigh far too heavy for me to shrug off
this intrusion into the previously safe and peaceful space
around me. My heart pounds, and this, this is my first
experience of terror in the canyons.

And this is how quickly it passes. Moments later, a
realization bathes me in relief: No one will find me here;
no machine could make it through the quicksand, let
alone navigate the winding, narrow passage that I hiked
in my search for water. I breathe easier, but in solidarity
with the canyon feel indignation at its violation. More
moments pass. Gradually, my mental screen clears; the
interference caused by fear and adrenaline fades, then
disappears. I think how implausible it is that a human-
driven machine has made its way into this canyon.
Remember the long and steep hike in. Remember -- and
savor -- the absence of signs of humans. Remember our
guide's words, that these canyons are managed as
wilderness. "Managed as wilderness" -- a statement as
reassuring now as it is absurd, the essence of wilderness
being the antithesis of "managed." But it does mean no
off-road vehicles, no bulldozers bent on rearranging the
Earth. A few moments pass. Suddenly, the proverbial
lightbulb goes on, no electricity needed. The sound IS

human-made, but it's not mechanical. Instead, it's me. I am the machine, and the sound I hear is the rushing of my own blood as it courses through my veins and arteries. My own internal stream, running even redder than the turbulent creek beyond. Not once before, in nearly 40 years, can I remember hearing it this way. Pulsing -- literally, and figuratively. I listen a moment longer to the quiet roaring inside my head as it crests, subsides, crests, subsides . . . check my watch, then make my way slowly back to the puddle in the rock. Luckily, there's enough water left in the bag that I can trust once again in the integrity of the output tube, in the safety of the filtered water soon to be flowing out its end into my 2-gallon container. I pour out the iodized water, taking care to aim far from that crystal-clear puddle, and prepare to pump again. This time, the tube will not pop out. I'll make sure of it, even though the afternoon sun has begun to tire me, and the hike back to my campsite will surely take longer than did the hike in.

Just as writing the story of the Voice is taking longer. Longer than what? I ask myself, back on the East coast again, facing my computer's glare head-on. Longer than I might have hoped? Longer than I might unreasonably have expected? Longer than the quest itself? Yes and no, to that one. Longer than 11 days, to be sure. But longer than the rest of my life? Hopefully not. Besides, the Voice hasn't finished talking yet, so how could I be finished writing?

Chapter 7

*"From wilderness we learned purity, learned to
listen to the voices that could only be heard with
the heart, not the ears."*

-- Tom Brown Jr., *The Vision*

Returning to my power spot on that first day,
carrying what I hoped was a 3-days' supply of water, I
saw again a flash of my own face as it had appeared to
me that morning -- reflected not in a mirror, not in the
eyes of fellow questers, but rather in the bright shiny
surface where memory takes on life. Immersed in a last-
minute check of my gear, I'd had a sudden image of
myself as a pigtailed child -- a child who'd grown up to be
very much afraid, beneath an exterior of calm and com-
petence. A child who, spontaneity shamed out of her by
school and grown-ups and culture, had learned to seek
shelter in boundaries and rules. Yet this morning, on the
threshold of what was arguably the most daring and
boundary-less journey of my life, that pigtailed child was,
incredibly, not afraid. Instead, she was smiling a broader,
lighter smile than the grown-up me had ever before
imagined. That child was delighted, she was happy, she
seemed so very grateful that 30-odd years later, this
older version of herself had decided to come to these
beautiful redrock canyons. And seeing that face, the

adult I had grown into smiled right back.

That's how the child I once had been had helped me to feel less afraid of shouldering my pack and hiking off alone. How the child who lived inside me had allowed me to acknowledge the adventure, and be exhilarated instead of incapacitated by it. And how, that evening, the child within was able to recognize the face of red fox in the creases and crevices and shadows of the far canyon wall, and hold that comforting image in my mind's eye in that in-between space, when vestiges of all daylight were gone, and the canyon wall was not yet illuminated by the moon. Red fox. One of my favorite animals as a child -- and now, my spirit guide to the south, where, symbolically, my inner child resides. But that's another chapter of the story . . . Suffice it to say that the first time the Voice came to me in the canyons, it wore the broad smile and trusting eyes of a child not-yet betrayed.

"*It's been dark for almost one and a half hours,*" I wrote in my journal. "*The moon is behind me, lighting up the canyon wall. Stars are everywhere. I'm cold, and I can't wait to crawl into my sleeping bag. Yet I remember Bill quoting Rumi -- 'don't go back to sleep'! I remember, too, my experience with the deep imagery two days ago at the grotto -- falling asleep, and realizing that sleep will be a nemesis of mine on this quest. My tarp tempts me, too, but I'd be so cut off from the sky. I'll sleep outside the tarp tonight, under the stars.*

"*What am I afraid of? Nothing to fear in the wilderness, except maybe rough weather. What I must be afraid of is fear itself. Too many fears, too long.*"

I did sleep under the stars that night -- fitfully, on just enough of a slope to keep my sleeping bag in a perpetual slow slide off my Therm-a-Rest pad toward a bush full of brambles, dreaming of confronting the darkness -- and was not, I repeat, was not afraid.

Chapter 8

*"How did the shadow disappear from our pursuit
of the light?"*

-- Margaret Wheatley, "Consumed by Fire or
Fire"

The next morning I awoke around 7, lying in my
sleeping bag and watching the sky and canyons
gradually lighten. I trusted that I was facing east, and so
waited in a soft and cozy state of semi-wakefulness for
the sun to rise over the facing ridge, to bathe me in its
healing warmth. Nights in the desert canyons can be
cold, even in October, and my allegedly warm-to-20-
degrees sleeping bag had failed the test at 40; on this
third morning of my fast, incredibly, I found myself
craving sunlight even more than food. But apparently,
my sense of direction had failed me during my
reconnaissance in the rain two days before. The longer I
waited for the sun and the farther away sleep wandered,
the clearer reality became: I was facing north, not east.
North. A 90-degree miscalculation, its results

measurable in lost degrees Fahrenheit and shade that
clung greedily to the landscape around me, loosening its
cool hard grip only hours after the last canyon wren gave
up its sweet-trilling morning serenade.

In contrast to the solar-heated rock of my imagination, this spot, it turned out, would receive direct sunlight only several hours each day. The rest of the time,
my teeth would be nearly chattering and I'd be wearing
every layer of clothing I had -- long underwear beneath
shorts, beneath long fleece pants; two long-underwear
shirts topped by a t-shirt, a wool sweater, a fleece vest
and, especially but not exclusively at night, a Gore-Tex
jacket with hood and a fleece hat and mask. Bathed, as it
were, not in sunlight but in shadow.

Chapter 9

> *"It should not be believed that all the beings exist for humanity. On the contrary, all the other beings too have been intended for their own sakes, and not for the sake of something else."*
>
> -- Moses Maimonides, medieval Jewish philosopher
>
> *"Tell me now my brothers Tell me now my sisters Who speaks for Wolf?"*
>
> -- Paula Underwood, "Who Speaks for Wolf"

It was that morning when a voice -- was it The Voice, or simply my voice? -- began, in honor of the Lakota, to lament. Resigned eventually to the chill, and no longer willing to wait for the sun lying down, I wriggled my body in its sleeping bag cocoon into a seated position overlooking the canyon, fresh and cleansed by its night-bath. From there, I began to sing, to chant, to ask Great Spirit over and over again the grandmother of all questions, "Why?"

There are countless permutations to that question, and what I found is that they -- like us -- are all related. Linked by some intangible, invisible thread, the why's of my own life (Why do I feel so sad? Why am I so afraid? Why can't I see more clearly the purpose of my life? Why did I choose a spot facing North?) merged into the why's of my family's life, into the why's of my friends' lives, into the why's of all the people who'd come before me and those who had yet to follow, into the why's of all the Earth's creatures, and finally into the why's of the Earth itself.

Like a rope that lies coiled until an anchor, dropped into the depths, unravels it quick and sure, no chance of slowing, so these why's tumbled faster and faster from my lips, outpacing the ability of my mind to anticipate them, rushing headlong and clamoring toward the chance to be given voice. Why, Great Spirit, why is there so much suffering? So much unhappiness? So much cruelty and abuse? Why, Great Spirit, have you allowed us to lose our connections to one other? To the Earth? To living beings other than ourselves? How, Great Spirit, have humans come to think that everything exists for their own use or their abuse? How could anyone possibly look at these canyons and not be moved? Not be humbled? Not feel love and not feel loved? Why would anyone prefer to see drilling rigs where the cottonwoods now stand? Think the only good wolf is a dead wolf? Fail to understand that we, too, are part of a greater plan? Why, Great Spirit, have you allowed so much of the Earth to be raped and wasted at the thoughtless hands of man? So many living creatures -- human and otherwise -- to be slaughtered, at the thoughtless hands of man?

Those why's battered my heart, and the ache of it rose up into my throat and it, too, took voice and flew away. But the why that finally made me cry surprised me. "Why, Great Spirit, why did I have to be born white?" My tears fell. "I am so ashamed of being white."

Chapter 10

> *"The belief that the Western way has been the best seems to me to be the shape of a madness that has been turned around and stated as logic and rationality . . .Where is the logic, we Indian women are asking, in the extinction of species, in deforestation that takes away our air, in emptying the sustaining oceans. What's being lost is almost everything, including our own lives."*

> -- Linda Hogan, "First People"

A year earlier. I stretch my legs and reluctantly sit down again on a too-hard too-narrow chair in one of those nondescript, windowless meeting rooms with vaguely stale air and glaringly unreal lighting that could be anywhere. This particular one, though, is in Washington, D.C., where I'm attending a conference on children's environmental health. I'm a writer and an activist and a teacher and a former public health educator. I'm not a physician and I'm not a scientist, though lots of people in the room are one or both; and the presenters know their audience. I'm learning a lot nonetheless -- mostly, that there's a prodigious amount of scientific evidence to support what I've intuitively known: the mind-boggling array of chemicals we've released into the environment is taking its toll, especially on children. Asthma. Cancer. The numbers are

skyrocketing, yet we're still unleashing more chemicals
to join all the old chemicals to brew even more-toxic
soups. I sigh. Wait for the next presentation to start and
hope for something to wake me up -- literally, not figuratively, the latter's already having been accomplished.

I am not disappointed. This presentation is by
SUNY Albany and its partners on the Akwesasne
Mohawk reservation, which straddles the U.S. / Canada
border. Instead of employing the slides and high-tech
laser pointers to which I've grown accustomed, these
presenters transport us into their very lives. They speak
to us of the St. Lawrence River, a waterway so polluted
that the Mohawk had to give up fish, the traditional
mainstay of their diet. Who knows this better than Katsi
Cook, a traditional midwife who has overseen a project to
gather data on the health effects of pollution on her
tribe's children? But Katsi doesn't feed us numbers;
instead, she feeds our souls. She sings to us in her native
tongue. I start to cry. I cry the whole time she sings. I cry
so hard that it takes tremendous effort not to sob out
loud. She finishes, and I'm still crying. People stand up
and stretch and some walk down in front to talk with
Katsi and the other presenters. I want to go, but I'm crying too hard to talk. I have no idea why.

Three years earlier. I'm taking a weeklong workshop at a conference called the Rainbow Connection. The
facilitator is an Irish American woman who's been
adopted by the Lakota. Looking past her ancestry and
recognizing her soul, Lakota elders have shared with her
their ancient knowledge and sacred ways. She is now a
medicine woman, a red-haired bridge between two
worlds. Today, she asks us to lie on the ground, face-
down, spread-eagle, and to allow ourselves to fully feel,
to feel the pain of the Earth. I've been conscious of that
pain for a long long time. Twenty years ago or more, my

heart broke at the photo of an oil-drenched duck on the cover of a magazine. In eighth grade I started an anti-pollution club, corresponding roughly with the first Earth Day. I've been an environmental reporter. I've been a crusader. I've walked in the ocean waves for hours, lain on the banks of the Delaware, hiked on the Appalachian Trail until my then-broken heart could mend. But none of that has prepared me for what I feel today. My body shakes slightly, and deep inside I feel a hollow yowling desperate grief. I lie there for a few moments and then get up slowly, feeling dazed. I can't lie there anymore -- the grief is big enough to swallow me -- but I am unwilling, at first, to move away. I feel shell-shocked. I am way too numb to cry.

Four years earlier. Flying home from Belize. I've just spent eight days in one of the most beautiful places imaginable. Four of the eight, in the midst of an unexcavated Mayan village hidden deep in a seasonal rainforest, the pyramids buried beneath centuries of dirt and secrets, camouflaged by ferns and trees. To get there, we flew for 45 minutes in a ridiculously small plane over forest that stretched from horizon to horizon, home to jaguar, to parrot, to howler monkey, to toucan. Now I sit in a large plane flying over the eastern United States. Below me, the land is carved into squares; wolf and mountain lion are gone. I stare out the window and feel sick -- not motion-sick, but sick at the contrast between the worlds. This land is but a shadow of itself; land is alive, and we in the western world have strangled it. My heart breaks, but instead of crying I try to figure out how changing my life -- transforming anger and sadness into action -- could help to change the world's.

Five years earlier. I am at my first pow-wow. It's in New Jersey, only an hour and a half from my home. I stand waiting for the grand entry, camera at the ready.

The drumming starts and the dancers enter, graceful, with great dignity, traditional costumes brilliant in the mid-day sun. I raise my camera to my eye, but I can't focus because I'm crying. Luckily, I have sunglasses on that hide my tears; I feel ashamed, and wonder whether any of the dancers notice. I cry for a long time. I cry until the opening closes. I have no idea why.

Many years earlier. I'm in junior high school. Frustrated by a curriculum that teaches about white European history that feels so ancient as to be almost mind-numbing, I feel drawn to learn about Native Americans. I borrow *Bury My Heart at Wounded Knee* from a mail-order library. The book chronicles in great detail the massacre of Native Americans by white Europeans, and the deliberate near-destruction of the rich and colorful mosaic of Native culture and spirituality. Several weeks pass, and I send it back without reading it. I couldn't tell you why.

Second day of my solo in The Canyon. I still haven't read *Bury My Heart at Wounded Knee*, but I know most of what it says from having read countless other books, watched documentaries, listened to Native speakers. I know, too, that the war on indigenous people isn't over; it continues in the rainforests of South America, in discriminatory public policies, and in battles over land and the "resources" on and below it, all around the globe. I know that the reason I haven't read *Bury My Heart at Wounded Knee* is that I haven't been able to bear it. But I also know that I'm personally blameless. So why do I feel a shame so intense that my tears nearly blind me? I have only half an idea why.

Chapter 11

> *"Whatever it is you think you are, give it up.*
> *There are powers at play in the world about*
> *which you know very little."*
>
> -- David Whyte

That afternoon, I carried my camp chair back to Lizard Rock and settled in to write in my journal about a dream the night before. *"I'm with Terry Williams* (a volatile bully of a man, who pretends to be kind and even-tempered) *and he's attempting to put me to sleep -- make me lose consciousness -- by using a hold like the neck squeeze from the original Star Trek series. He's trying to be cool and calm, so I won't realize what he's doing. But I do, and I fight back. Now he's naked (exposed) and I'm kicking him. It seems I am 'winning.'"* Some dreams are complex but still fathomable; others, a complete mystery. This one seemed fairly simple: The darkness tries to fool us -- put us to sleep -- but sometimes we stay awake. Sometimes we fight against evil. And sometimes we even win.

Later: *"Just took apart my whole daypack looking for grouse feather, to no avail. Talked aloud, telling feather I missed her -- and, if it wouldn't be against feather's nature to live with me, I'd love to have her back.*

44

Otherwise, I honor and respect feather's decision to leave.
After all, who wouldn't want to live here in The Canyon?"

Later still, I looked up from my journal to see a
lizard -- this one, unlike the rock, sized to scale and
breathing -- skittering across the loose sand and
disappearing somewhere in the vicinity of my crossed
hiking boots. A few moments passed before I cautiously
moved the toe of one boot just in time to see lizard
clamber down from the other and scurry off under the
sagebrush. Moments later, he was back. Climbed right
back up onto the toe of my boot and sat there watching
me, a tall 12 inches closer to my eye level -- until I
sneezed once (he stayed there), twice (riding out the
storm), and then again (Enough already!). He scampered
down off my boot, but this time, stopped short of the
sagebrush. Instead, he rested in the sand just a foot or so
away, watching, albeit more warily now.

I talked to him. Thanked him for being, and for
being there, keeping me company. In my not-quite-
ordinary state of mind (two days and nights without food
were starting to have an effect, so subtle I would have
denied it), I treated my encounter with lizard as totally
ordinary. Accepted uncritically his trust in me, a strange
reclining giant, didn't think to question his two-times
climb to the tip of a boot that could so easily have
crushed him. And then I was shaken by an especially
powerful fit of sneezing; when my vision cleared, lizard
was gone.

"*I'm having a powerful allergy attack right now*," I
wrote in my journal. "*Can't stop sneezing, my eyes itchy
and watery. I'm sitting at the very same spot as this
morning, when I didn't sneeze at all.*" Why am I sneezing
now? The only answer I received was the harsh echo of
yet another sneeze, barking back at me from across the
canyon.

Chapter 12

> *"The experience of fear is physical. It is neither imaginary nor conceptual, but is known directly through the body."*
>
> -- Laura Simms, "Through the Story's Terror"

Ah-choo!!!! Another sneeze explodes. This time -- the second time I have a full-fledged confrontation with Fear in the canyons -- it is visceral, nearly crippling. Not the result of strange sounds, and, like the first time, not at night. Instead, Fear again chooses an afternoon of bright blue skies and clouds wispy as a waking dream. And, as often happens, Fear sneaks up on me, clothed in the innocuous: yet another sneeze, and an itch initially so subtle that I probably scratch it four or five or 15 times before it makes its way to consciousness. By the time it does, however, "subtle" is no longer an accurate descriptor of either the sneezes or the itch. "*Damn!*," I write. "*Another allergy attack. Virtually non-stop sneezing. None of this happened yesterday -- why today? Beings can probably hear my sneezes all the way up and down the canyon. Now my right eye itches terribly. Is this the way spirit worked out to wear down my ego?*"

Our group of questers had been warned: Beware the ego, that logical, rational, shamelessly domineering part of you, the part that thinks and plots and plans, the part that wants you to believe it's the whole of you. It will conspire to distance you from your experience, from the canyons, from your hunger and your pain; it will spew out a never-ending stream of thoughts to distract you. Ego is fighting for its own survival, so it will be ruthless. And, it will try everything to cut you off from the Voice of Soul, from the Voice of Great Spirit.

The ego, I realized later, would never have admitted to shame at being white because, after all, I am. Just the kind of situation that is anathema to the control-hungry ego -- one of utter powerlessness. And so, ego would exert the only kind of "power" it could -- the power to deny feelings about a situation over which it had no power. Obviously, then, my ego had already begun to lose its grip on the morning of my lament in The Canyon. Now, it was about to fall.

"My ass itches horribly, too. What IS this about?" Feeling the first hint of panic, I focus intently on the machinations of my rational mind, the intellect that has served me well so often, and ponder my own question:

Obviously, I think, "what this is about" is an allergic reaction. But to what? Pollen? Maybe. But how would that relate to my ass? It couldn't. OK. Have I done anything unusual? More unusual than camping alone in an isolated canyon, I mean? Have I done anything I didn't do yesterday, or even two hours ago? Yes!, I think, my mind spinning faster. The sun finally shone on my spot a short while ago, so I took off my long underwear! Maybe I had something on my hands that irritated my skin!? Or perhaps there's some irritant in the lining of my shorts, which are touching bare skin for the first time since I bought them? Of course! That must be it . . .

And so, on the basis of that which my mind has "figured out," I do two things. I put my long underwear back on, but only after using precious filtered water to rinse my hands of irritants, be they actual or imagined, and I cover my nose with a mask of toilet paper. Toilet paper: a sadly ineffectual filter. But then, the possibility of an airborne irritant is quite slim; covering my nose with toilet paper is more to help me feel that I am taking every possible precaution. To help me feel, quite incorrectly, that I'm "in control."

"*Have small welts, like bug bites, on my sides where my shorts fit over my hips,*" I write after re-donning my long underwear. "*All around my waist, incredibly itchy welts,*" I add a few short minutes later. "*Put Polysporin on the welts -- not effective at all. Also checked my face to make sure I didn't have hives. I don't. So now, I wait for the itching to stop. My blood is pounding so hard in my ears, it feels like they're moving. My tongue feels odd, too. Soon I'll have to look at it in the mirror. Of course, why would I get hives in my mouth? I've taken nothing internally. . . Did check my tongue -- all seems fine. But my ass, walking from the tarp* (where I went to fetch a small hand mirror), *felt like it had burrs in it.*"

A few moments later: "*Welts on my lower legs, too. God, why didn't I bring an antihistamine?*" A few moments later still: "*Holy shit! Unbelievable welts on my hips -- huge! I guess I'll wait a few hours and see how they are. If no better, I could always return to base camp and see if anyone has an antihistamine. I keep checking on my tongue -- it feels odd, but looks OK.* (I knew that allergic reactions can make tongues swell, sometimes interfering with the ability to swallow or to breathe.)

"*So, what IS this about? I'm scared, now -- scared that I'm having some bizarre allergic reaction that could kill me. 'Dying' to my current life in order to be reborn is one thing, but literally dying is something else! I'm going to see what happens in the next hour . . . God, if only I'd brought a Benadryl . . .*"

Chapter 13

> *"If the desert is holy, it is because it is a forgotten*
> *place that allows us to remember the sacred.*
> *Perhaps that is why every pilgrimage to the*
> *desert is a pilgrimage to the self. There is no*
> *place to hide, and so we are found."*
>
> -- Terry Tempest Williams, *Refuge: An*
> *Unnatural History of Family and Place*

What happened in the next hour was this: I tried to fight panic, and failed. And then, I realized I really truly did not want to die. My will to live was so strong, in fact, that I was willing to do several things I would normally have avoided at almost any cost: admit my vulnerability; ask for help from someone other than a long-trusted friend or lover; and potentially inconvenience others. Worst-case scenarios collided in my fear-drunk brain, and I wondered whether I'd need medical help beyond what the guides could offer; whether I'd have to hike out for help; whether, worst-case scenario of all, we'd all have to hike out, just because of me. *What if everyone's quest has to end, on account of me?* Amazingly, I realized I'd do it anyway; I'd hike back to base camp to ask for help. And I'd do it now. Worst-case closed.

Of course hiking back to base camp was going to require stamina that only adrenaline could bring. I hadn't eaten for 2½ days, and my energy level was low. The afternoon sun was out full-force, and it was bound to be hot on the canyon floor. I filled my water bottle, made sure that my emergency supplies were in my pack, and realized that I'd left my pouch back under Lizard Rock. My lapis point, a rune carved with the symbol for "strength", a piece of coral from a favorite beach in the Caribbean, a fossil given to me as good luck by an 8-year-old, a crystal leant to me by a friend -- all of these were in my pouch. I needed all the help I could get, and so I took a short detour back toward Lizard Rock to get it.

On the way, I glanced down -- as I must have done at least 25 times in the past day and a half -- and marveling, stopped short. I couldn't believe what my eyes were seeing: grouse feather! Lying there on the path to Lizard Rock, waiting to be found. It was nothing short of a miracle, and I knew it. There was no logical reason for that feather to be there, considering the intense wind that had buffeted The Canyon on the evening of the day I'd dropped it. And there also was no logical reason I hadn't found it earlier. How could I have walked this path so many times before, and each time failed to see? Had Feather been there all the time? Or had it just now rematerialized, back, perhaps, from wherever unattached feathers go to restore their gift of flight? Had Feather -- or someone, at least, some spirit or helper or perhaps my own soul, working her magic in cahoots with The Canyon -- been moved by my earlier plea? I didn't know the answer, but as I stooped down to pick up Feather I did know something important -- I was, and would be, fine. I was not meant to die here in this canyon.

Yet I still set off for base camp, to be absolutely sure.

Chapter 14

*"The human shape is a ghost made of distraction
and pain. Sometimes pure light, sometimes cruel,
trying wildly to open, this image tightly held
within itself."*

-- Jelaluddin Rumi (translated by John Moyne &
Coleman Barks)

I'd been right -- it was hot. But having lived
mostly in the shadows for the past 1½ days, I hadn't realized the awesome power of a blazing desert sun. I started
out wearing most of my layers; by the time I lost sight of
my power spot I'd already removed two of them. My
backpack of survival gear -- water, emergency
whistle, "emergency blanket" a.k.a. ineffectual piece of
lightweight foil, sized for a human instead of a sandwich
-- grew more bulky with each piece of clothing I discard-
ed. Eventually, I spotted Tracey. She was sitting in the
sun by the mouth of the side canyon where her power
spot was, and she looked up with great surprise to see
me. I didn't feel like talking, so I just asked for a
Benadryl. She didn't have one. Further upstream I
encountered an apprentice guide named Terry, writing in
his journal. Got a Benadryl? He didn't, either. Speaking
with them seemed incongruous; I'd adjusted quickly to a
world within, a world without distraction, so that the

strange had become familiar and the previously familiar, strange. I kept walking toward base camp; with each step I took, my feet grew heavier. With each "no" I heard in response to my request for Benadryl, I felt more and more like crying. Yet for some reason, I didn't. Raven soared above, his call beating me up the canyon by at least 10 city blocks.

By the time I reached base camp, my layers had been peeled away one by one by one. There a guide and an apprentice listened to my story and peered compassionately at the welts forming an angry circle around my hips. Dianne, the guide, said that sizing in clothing could cause allergic reactions similar to mine. She also told me the second chakra, where the hives had concentrated, is associated with feelings and emotions. Associated, in other words, with the very substance of a quest. Not surprising that the welts would show up there, bringing me, apparently, some message. But what was it?

As I talked with them I grew calmer; I could see, too, that the hives had begun to fade. Patti, the apprentice, gave me the antihistamine I'd sought so desperately; I tucked it into my pocket but was almost sure now that I wouldn't need it. Dianne gave me a homeopathic remedy for stress, the bitter taste of drops on my tongue an oddly welcome sensation. But most of all, they both gave me their loving attention. And so, heartened, I turned around and began the long slow hike back to my solo spot.

The whole way there I felt, again, the insistent urge to cry, tempered not at all, it seemed, by the knowledge that the hives were disappearing; exacerbated, perhaps, by the still-strange yet oh-so-welcome realization that I'd loved myself enough to ask for help. Despite my exhausted eagerness to get back "home," I overshot my spot. Found myself further downstream, the trees and rocks looking eerily unfamiliar. I turned around again, disorientation and fatigue increasing with each blink of the eyes, the blinks coming more frequently, reaction to perspiration, a manifestation of one perplexed. The sun no longer just beat down on me, but beat me down.

I walked even more slowly, stepped even more deliberately. Looked for landmarks. The problem was, viewed from the opposite direction everything looked different. It was like seeing the backs of familiar store-fronts, all looking confusingly alike with their dumpsters and their parking lots and their dingier-than-the-front-door doors. Yet it was not like that at all, for nothing here was dirty, nothing carved into mind-numbing order by the controlling hand of man. It was like driving home in dense fog, and not recognizing your own driveway.

After what seemed like too many steps -- had I passed my site again, missing the obvious as I'd apparently missed grouse feather? -- I glimpsed out of the corner of my eye the glaring blue of my tarp, and this welcome vision, I knew, was no mirage. I turned toward it, gratefully. Dragged myself up the steep entrance to my spot, where I collapsed, breathing hard, onto my Therma Lounger. Where I discovered that I had my menstrual period, one week early -- literal blood to match the figurative bleeding that already had begun. Where, finally, I allowed myself to cry. (Or when, perhaps, I no longer had the energy not to.)

Journal entry, 5 p.m.: "*Sobbed for a long time. Started crying when I told Great Spirit how scared I'd been (and, to some degree, still was). Never before in my life have I had hives -- or such an intense allergic reaction. Even my spot -- my beautiful power spot -- feels somewhat threatening now. I guess the truth is, I want to be home!*"

Earth Dreams

Four more hours passed. I sat on my chair, watching the immovable canyon walls. Felt the cramps that, this time, couldn't be calmed by drugs, ibuprofen on an empty stomach not advisable. Sank deeper into an unwelcome, first-time-in-the-canyons feeling of not belonging: not belonging to the ruggedly beautiful landscape suddenly turned alien, the site fear had chosen to write its signature across my skin; not belonging on the quest (just as sure as I was wrong, that no one else was feeling so down and so defeated); and not -- definitely not -- belonging to a world in which the Voice constantly whispered wisdom beyond words and spread comfort like starlight on a bright and cloudless night.

Journal entry, 8:40 p.m.: "*I am almost desperate to go to sleep. Was momentarily comforted by the stars, but now a lot are obscured by clouds. I hate being here right now. I feel like I'd give anything to be home, clean and cuddled in my nice warm bed. But would I give the chance to be fully alive for the rest of my life? Probably not. . . The truth is, though, I'm miserable. I'm hungry, very tired, worried about the weather, worried that I won't have enough tampons to get me through, and -- most importantly -- feeling hopeless and defeated. Of course, I remember our guide saying LET YOURSELF BE DEFEATED. So, is this a GOOD thing? Sure doesn't feel that way. Feels terrible. TERRIBLE! Right now I wonder how I can make it through another day (and night!). I could be thinking -- ah! half over, and the fast, more than half . . . But it all feels like too much right now. Too damned much! I know I am strong, and brave. But THIS SUCKS! BIGTIME! Some creature is crying right now, and sounds to be coming closer. Haven't a clue what it is. . . Now it's stopped. 9 p.m. I'm going to get under the tarp.*" And I did, and slept fitfully but warmly, in contrast to the prior night.

Chapter 15

> *"The only thing left for human beings to do, in a universal sense, is to find ways of ridding themselves of boredom. What they end up doing is finding ways of killing time: the only commodity no one has enough of."*
>
> -- don Juan, in *Magical Passes* by Carlos Castaneda

"*1*0/10 -- the last day of my solo. 9:15 a.m. Got up only about 30 minutes ago. Today is a mix of blue sky and many large clouds, most of them white but a few dark gray. I have an itch on my side, but too many layers of clothing to get to it. Also, my urine stinks like a skunk. I could spend lots of time (well, not lots -- my only reference is the first aid checklist from the vision quest manual) trying to figure out why, but that would be my ego again. Stinky urine isn't going to kill me, and in less than 24 hours I'll be back at base camp and eating again (!). It was much warmer sleeping under the tarp last night . . . Still didn't sleep well, though -- and no dreams that I remember. . .

"There's a small bug sitting on my arm -- has been for a while now. I talk to it, but if it answers, I can't hear."

What about the Voice? If the Voice spoke to me, would I hear? And if I sang to the Voice, would the Voice respond? For the rest of the morning, I sat overlooking the canyon, singing, chanting, praying, rattling. Many of the words were repetitive, so that I barely thought of them at all -- "Oh Great Spirit I am calling you, Oh Earth Mother what else can I do? Open me up, that I might receive, open me up that I might believe," sung over and over again; other words, like those that had brought me face to reddened face with shame at the legacy of my white skin, took me by surprise. They came from somewhere not quite conscious, and they asked in many different ways for guidance. But to say that I heard the Voice respond would be a lie. If the Voice did answer me that morning, it did so quietly, by silencing the nagging of fear and doubt, by allowing me to ride the waves -- the wake of the previous night's angry exhaustion -- to a calmer place, by allowing me to settle into the present.

"1:25 p.m. Feel MUCH better today," I wrote in my journal. *"Clear that I'll stay up all night. Clouds are the ultimate shape-shifters. Off now to dig a fire pit."*

And I did. Using a rock and my hands, wet clumps of sand bulging from under fingernails, blurring the boundary between body and Earth, I scraped out an area down in the creekbed that was six inches deep and scarcely larger in diameter. Around it, I built a "purpose circle" -- a ceremonial circle marked by stones for each of the four directions, and at its center, beautiful rock of dark red chert and crystalline quartz. When darkness fell, I planned to be seated there; when the morning sun sent pink light and wispy clouds to soften the sky for its arrival, I planned to be seated there still. In between, a night of ceremony, of watching the stars and moon make their way across the sky. Night of reverence; morning of new beginnings. But oh god was I tired now. So tired that for brief moments, my mind was still. So tired that when I did think of it, I hadn't a clue how tired I really was.

"*3 p.m. Amazing that the fast hasn't left me spacier and even weaker than I am! Feel like all I'm doing right now is waiting -- waiting 'til it's time to go to the purpose circle and stay up all night. . . Will I have a vision? Right about now, the main vision I'm having is of food. . .*

"*4:40 p.m. Raven flew directly overhead -- so close I could hear the beating of his wings . . . There are quite a few flies around, buzzing me and sitting on me. I try to be mindful of what our guide said -- say YES! to everything. It sure is tough with flies. Occasionally I instinctively shoo one -- and even, a few times, by intent . . .*

"*Lots of clouds off to the west, but so far none seem threatening. Very dense, however. I think they're moving north, which means they'll bypass me. I'm feeling hungrier now -- maybe it's the anticipation of tomorrow morning, and food (!!!!!!!) Then, the next day, shower. HO! Maybe, to be on the safe side, I'll stuff my sleeping bag and put it in the pack in the plastic bag. I realize that if it blew and rained hard, my tarp wouldn't be sufficient.*"

And with that utilitarian entry, the journal of my solo experience in the wilderness abruptly ended.

Chapter 16

"Fight to stay awake. Choose the path you take.
Even if you don't know where it's going."

-- Jan Garrett, "Don't Go Back to Sleep"

It's not that I didn't have anything more to write about. My journal writing ended because I fell asleep -- not literally, but in the much more deadening sense of a Rumi poem:
"The breeze at dawn has secrets to tell you.
   Don't go back to sleep.
You must ask for what you really want.
   Don't go back to sleep.
People are going back and forth across the doorsill
   where the two worlds touch.
The door is round and open.
   Don't go back to sleep."
Going back to sleep, at least as I understand Rumi, means drifting away from the present. It means closing down the portals between oneself and the world. It means losing awareness, "checking out", "spacing out" . . . and missing out. And it virtually always means assuming oneself awake.
   So rather than lie down to sleep off this empty

"sleep", which at least would have afforded me the chance to dream, I walked slowly to the tarp, crawled awkwardly underneath, stuffed my sleeping bag, placed it in the bottom of my backpack, placed the backpack in the middle of the ground-cloth, covered it with a plastic bag, crawled awkwardly out, and retied the edges of the tarp to make ready my camp for rain. Then I sat down again, counting the hours until sundown.

Later -- how much later, I couldn't really say -- I made my way carefully down to the creekbed, placed my chair in the center of the purpose circle, and sat down with a sigh as heavy as my hiking boots the day their soles were clogged with quicksand. As heavy as my head felt, crammed full of sluggishly moving images and hazy thoughts that began but never ended, curling atop and around and under themselves, weaving a messy ball of meaninglessness. That sigh attested to what this magical experience had somehow become -- tedious, and empty as the breath at the far end of a long exhale. For in going back to sleep, my spirit had temporarily left me. In its place was a body going through the motions . . . through motions such as these:

    * Building a fire after the darkness finally came -- a fire in which, symbolically, I'd planned to burn 40 twigs gathered from the gnarled and ancient juniper and from the ground on which they'd been strewn by wind or rain or time, a twig for each year of my life to date. Each one, representing an aspect of who I was. Some, representing the roles I played in a world infatuated with labels, categories, titles -- a world fluent in the language of separateness, not of connectedness or grace. The bright orange coals left by these discarded selves would be something to contemplate deeply until, finally, they faded to nothing and were covered by me, shrouded by the sand. In the wake of their fiery exit could enter my true

self, my own authentic voice crying out with joy, with
passion, without subterfuge, without fear of
judgment from the silently witnessing Canyon.

Yet the sand was damp, my waterproof matches
nearly strike-proof, my patience nearly gone, my pissed-
off ego (angered at having been left, albeit briefly, in the
background) waiting just behind the cottonwood for an
excuse to express its rage. First strike of a match:
Nothing. Second strike: Nothing. Third strike: Success!
But the wind, which I hadn't noticed before, blew out the
flame before I had a chance to lower it to the loose pile of
dried grass and twigs I had so carefully amassed. Fourth
strike: The same. Fifth strike: The same. Sixth strike: I
managed to keep the match lit until it ignited one of the
twigs. But the spark was short-lived, followed by a quiet
hiss, then nothing. Seventh strike: The same. Eighth
strike: The same. Finally, it was my impatience that
caught fire. I gave up on the sticks. Instead, I struck
another match and held it to the corner of a letter I'd carried with me to the desert -- a letter as mean-spirited as
it was thorough in its brutal dissection of my life, a letter
from someone who supposedly loved me. I wanted to be
free of the weight of that letter, to stand tall beneath the
stars. The letter burned, spewing horrible, acrid smoke
that made my eyes water and threatened to choke me.
"Typical," I thought. I covered up the fire, and threw 37
twigs at the darkness.

* Angry flailing as I struggled against the wind to
wrap my chilled body in the so-called "emergency blanket" -- lightweight foil, sized for a human instead of a
sandwich and, I learned now, totally lacking the charm of
aluminum foil, its ability to be molded to a shape and
kept there. This supposedly space-age material *was* the
emergency, I decided -- flimsy, worthless, the invention of
some anti-Christ of camping, some enemy of wilderness

intent on killing off its champions one by excruciating one, frustrating them to the point of suicide or, in an actual emergency, leaving them cold. Sure enough, there was a part of me that could see the humor, could recognize the stuff of slapstick as I tucked the "blanket" around one side of my body, only to have it billow up and away from the other side, to be snatched back from the greedy wind, moments later to be snatched back by the greedy wind, until I had lost all semblance of control, cursing and grabbing and slapping ineffectually at a "blanket" that offered little additional warmth anyway. Mostly, though, I saw only aggravation; and my ego, a chance to vent its anger.

    * This motion, too, unique in a night of frayed nerves and scattered attention in that it combined mental concentration with physical coordination: The tiny bulb in my Maglite flashlight burned out, and I managed, somehow, to replace it with fingers turned thick and clumsy by the cold, my way lit only by the wavering light of a candle. Ah! Necessity, mother of intention. Sitting in a darkness so vast that it obliterated all memory of the sun, that compact flashlight provided far more comfort than it did light; and though I could live without the light (seeing by the stars and the moon that I hadn't disappeared), I could not, it seemed, live without the comfort. True, I had chosen to leave the flashlight off for long periods of time while I stared at the sky -- some-times seeing, sometimes not. But I'd known that at any moment, a simple twist of my fingers would allow me to exert some semblance of control, to create, if need be, a safe haven of light around me. And so I managed to cut through the sloppy wandering of my thoughts with a cold hard stab of logic; I knew what to do -- light the candle lantern; carefully remove the spare bulb from the base of the flashlight; banish the fears of dropping it; unscrew

the old bulb; screw in the new; steady my hands to do all of the above -- and I did it.

Finally, there was the sitting and the watching, head tilted back, noticing the movement of stars and moon. Seeing, with a flash of surprise and the only delight I experienced that seemingly endless night, one shooting star. Then another, and another. One, like I had never seen; similar to a firecracker, it exploded halfway across the sky. At 15 shooting stars, I quit counting.

Later, when the sky had already begun to lighten, black fading to a dark then lighter gray, I peered out through the slits of eyes too heavy to fully open and saw, off to my right, a gathering of native dancers. Not Native American, as far as I could tell, but African, stepping joyously, wearing festive costumes, a living celebration. But when I managed to open my eyes further, I saw only grasses, swaying. Later, I saw that the sky was really a giant tarpaulin, stretched taut over Grandmother Earth. Yet if you'd asked, I'd have told you nothing really happened that long cold night, and it would've been far better to have gone to sleep -- and I mean that literally.

Chapter 17

> *"Enter each day with the expectation that the happenings of the day may contain a clandestine message addressed to you personally."*
>
> -- Sam Keen

On the other hand, trudging back up to my tarp and going to sleep would have meant quitting. Giving up. Giving in. Much better to have wrested some modest benefit from this failed experiment of a spiritual experience by beating my desire to sleep. By doing what I'd set out to do, at least in the appearance of it, so that I could say I'd stayed up all night beneath the stars. So that I could give myself credit, at least, for that. And when morning finally came, the pastel colors of the dawn vanished in the blackness of my mood. It was as if the moon had done more than simply move across the sky that night; inside me, nearly four decades of suppressed rage and pain awakened with the dawn. Forget about dismantling my purpose circle, putting the rocks back where I'd found them. "Leave no trace" was fine and good, but I was exhausted. How the hell could I remember exactly where I'd found those rocks? I gathered my daypack and my chair, turned my back on the empty circle of my purpose, and began the weary climb back up to my campsite.

Earth Dreams

There, I moved in slow motion: first cutting the ropes tying my tarpaulin in place, then haphazardly stuffing everything in or onto my backpack, and then sliding the lot of it unceremoniously over the edge of the steep descent from my solo spot. I followed, sliding clumsily on my butt. Down below, I struggled to shoulder the pack and stand upright. When I'd recovered my balance, I walked off, ever so slowly, toward a rendezvous with my buddy.

But Tracey wasn't at the appointed spot for our meeting -- the stone pile, where the simple addition of one rock had spoken volumes to the other: "I'm OK," or, more accurately, "I was OK 6 or 10 or 14 hours ago, when I found this stone and placed it on top of yours." This morning, the morning that was supposed to mark our triumphant return to base camp, the morning when the worst was supposed to be over, Tracey wasn't there. And I, as annoyed as I was exhausted, kicked apart the stone pile. As with my purpose circle, I didn't even try to put the stones back where they'd originally lain. Never mind that I revered the Earth, or that, under normal circumstances, I would be the last one to knowingly leave a mark in the wilderness. This wasn't normal.

I checked my watch. Checked it again. Called out. Sweated. Decided, finally, to get rid of the backpack. Laboriously checked the contents of my daypack for water, the emergency whistle, the first aid instructions, and yes, the human-sized sandwich wrap. Then I turned in the direction of Tracey's solo spot and started walking, away from the main canyon and back a narrow winding side canyon. After all, something serious could have happened. She could have gotten hurt or sick. She could have grown disoriented. Maybe she merely overslept. Or, as turned out to be the case, she could simply have cared less about the time than I did. Just shy of the spot she'd

camped, Tracey and I met, turned toward the main
canyon and plodded out. She, much more lively than I. I,
making an effort to throttle my resentment. I'd had to
take that goddamned pack off and, worse still, put it on
again. That shouldn't have happened, had Tracey had
the decency -- or rigidity, I acknowledged later, a lifetime
later or so it seemed -- to be there at the time we'd
designated.

Fifteen minutes later, we walked into base camp.
There, the enthusiastic greeting of guides and apprentices seemed distant; their words, intended for someone
else. Sure, they looked at me when they spoke, they
smiled at me, they even hugged me. But I heard and saw
it all as if from the center of a void, and felt it, not at all.
Ironic, for I had looked forward to this moment for days
(three of them), had expected to feel exaltation, joy, a
sense of incredible accomplishment. Most important, a
sense of being fundamentally changed, and for the better.
A sense of having been reborn. Instead, I just felt tired; I
was alienated not only from them, it seemed, but also
from myself.

God, had going on this quest meant nothing? I'd
arrived in Colorado disconnected from life, and I'd
returned from my solo feeling disconnected from life. I
lowered myself wearily onto my chair, holding half an
avocado seasoned with cayenne pepper and garlic, and
ate. Even that held much less pleasure than I'd expected.
I watched my fellow questers make their way into camp,
two by two, saw the expressions on their faces, the light
in their eyes. They were strangers who'd slain dragons.
Strangers who'd communed with Spirit. Strangers who'd
talked to the soil at their feet and gotten answers,
returning giddy with the wonder of it. None of their
experiences had anything to do with me. And though I
sat in the center of everything, just as I had on the night

of the first campfire in The Canyon, still I sat alone.

Later, we ate sand. Not ceremonially, not purpose-fully, not even on purpose. In fact, we tried not to. But the sand clung to the inside of our cups and bowls, lent a gritty consistency to the stew that served as the second and final course of break-fast. There was sand, in fact, everywhere. The wind whipped us, and it whipped the sand, and then the sand whipped us too. I hadn't thought it possible to feel dirtier than I already did, but with sand in my mouth, sand in my hair, sand on exposed skin, sand gathering in the creases of my clothing, I realized I'd been wrong. Our guide checked his watch often, and saw a barometer falling fast. But no one panicked. Instead, we talked about rebuilding our camp-sites, for the plan was to stay in base camp the rest of the day and night. To share sacred stories, to engage in ceremony, to eat two more meals, to get a good -- exhausted, dead-as-a-doornail, dense-as-drugged -- sleep, to restore our strength for tomorrow's hike up and out of the canyon.

But plans can change. I sat, feeling myself grow more and more agitated. We should get out, now, I thought. What's wrong with our guides? How can they even think of making us rebuild our camps? How will we ever be able to tie down our tarpaulins, in this freaking wind? I felt weak despite the food now in my belly, and the thought of unpacking my pack was almost unbearable. But I got up, grudgingly, and followed my pre-solo campmates upstream to where we'd begin to make camp again. Until our guide called "Wait!" We turned, walked back. The guides and apprentices had huddled and made the very decision for which I'd hoped -- we would all hike out, today.

Chapter 18

Relief. I did feel that. Not having to make camp, being able to get out of this no-longer hospitable canyon, making it to "civilization" and a shower a full day ahead of schedule -- all these were like a cool breeze on a day of stifling heat and oppressive stillness. But I began to feel something else, as well, and that was fear. Hiking in had been hard. There'd been places where I'd glimpsed steep precipices just inches from my feet and felt cold sweat and queasiness -- the barely contained panic of someone long afraid of edges and of heights. There'd been times when the awkwardness of the backpack had caused me to stumble, 35 extra pounds seeming to sever accustomed ties between brain and feet, making my body dull and clumsy. There'd been moments when I'd wondered how I could manage to take another step.

And yet, I'd had a full night's sleep before the long hike in (today, I was on my 29th sleepless hour); behind me had stretched countless days of three rectangular meals (today, I was coming off a 4-day fast, and slowly);

and I'd been buoyed by excitement (today, there was only emptiness, and the vaguest sense of something lost). So if the hike in had been hard and scary, what about the hike out? My god, what about the hike out?!?

Meanwhile, the wind flung sand particles like tiny daggers against our faces. Less than an hour after breakfast, we ate a hurried lunch, most of us standing, our camp chairs dissembled and stowed in our packs, our packs covered with plastic garbage bags in anticipation of storms ahead. Peanut butter, rice cakes, sand, hummus, crackers, sand. Seeing the uncertainty in my eyes, a fellow quester recommended that I put dried fruit in my water bottle -- extra energy for the long hike out. I did, hoping for a miracle. And somehow, while lifting my pack, I twisted my leg. It hurt, caused me to walk with a barely perceptible limp. Mostly, though, it fed the ravenous monster that was my fear. I knew with a sickening, shameful certainty that I was not strong enough to hike out. And yet, I told no one. Inside, I was on the verge of tears. And yet, I showed no one. Instead, I got into line immediately behind our guide, who'd asked those who expected to keep the slowest pace to follow him so that he wouldn't walk too fast. One of the men tightened the straps of my backpack with abrupt yanks that stole my breath, left me feeling hollow as a reed, ready to break off at the next strong breeze. And then we started walking.

And that was how, 15 minutes later, I came to pass my solo spot, so tired and so dirty and so inexplicably angry that I barely glanced up at the place where I'd spent three days and nights alone. Grit in my mouth, every step a conscious act of balancing a 35-pound pack against a nearly incapacitating exhaustion and the ominous threat of a fast-falling barometer, I did tell myself over and over again that I could make it. I did try to bargain with myself -- or, perhaps more accurately, I berated myself, using the age of the oldest hiker to shame my 39-year-old body into keeping up the pace. I matched affirmations to my steps (I'm young, I'm strong, I can do this, I am doing this); with a grim dedication born of fear, I didn't miss a beat. We passed Anasazi ruins, just up and off to our left. Normally fascinated by the Anasazi, I barely looked up. A cold rain started, the sky a harbinger of the kind of weather that makes humans feel their vulnerability like a splinter jammed under a fingernail. I was too tired to care. When the group stopped for a break called by someone else, I felt like crying -- this time, in gratitude.

But only when we began our true ascent from the canyon -- when we had to take big steps onto higher rocks -- only then did my weakness become fully apparent. That's when I had to ask our guide to take my hand and pull me up. Otherwise, I wouldn't have made it. I hated to ask for help; hated to admit I needed it. But stronger than my resistance was my exhaustion and my fear. His distraction made me ask him twice. I complied. When he urged everyone to follow exactly in his footsteps, to avoid tramping on cryptobiotic soil -- that great life-giver of the desert, the essential ingredient in this gauntly beautiful landscape -- my anger burned. "You asshole. Can't you see that I'm barely hanging on?" (I thought but didn't say). "If I have to crush some god-damn crypto to save myself from falling off the edge of a cliff, I'll do it." And probably, I did.

Chapter 19

> *"One does not become enlightened by imagining figures of light, but by making the darkness conscious."*
>
> -- Carl Jung

Throughout the hike out, on the long car ride back to Durango (when I talked of books, of the politics of U.S. / Indian relations, of anything but the quest), and during the evening hours before a truly exhausted sleep, the darkness remained with me. A shower washed the grit from my body but had no effect whatsoever on the scummy ring around my heart. And yet still I told no one about my sadness or my pain. Why? Because of my shame, I realized later. Something about feeling frightened and negative and angry -- something about crashing head-first into the shadow side of the human experience and getting stuck there, mired like a school bus up to its wheelwells in mud -- had made me very much ashamed.

No surprise, I suppose. After all, my darkness was the mark of my failure. And failure is a shameful thing. I had failed at the quest. Failed to come out of the experience a better person than the one who'd gone in. Deep inside me, where I'd expected to find a clear connection to the light and to my sacred purpose, I'd found darkness.

I had failed at the quest.

Hadn't I?

It sure felt that way.

The next morning, the other questers' moods were light. Shortly, we'd all be meeting for an elders' council -- a ceremonial gathering that, had it not been for the sandstorm, would have occurred at base camp. At the council, one quester at a time would speak; the ears and hearts of 18 others would offer undivided, loving attention as the speaker told the story of his or her solo, and the gifts that came therein. I hadn't a clue what I was going to say. And I didn't cram, either, at least not in the sense of feverishly searching for some deep meaning that I could share. Instead, I focused all my attention on packing filthy sandy stinky clothing into my backpack so I wouldn't have to look at it again until I was home, standing in front of the washing machine, this whole stinking experience behind me. So in that sense only -- the literal sense of shoving more items into a backpack than by rights should have fit there -- did I cram. Not surprisingly, no great realizations came to me, though I did seriously consider throwing away my socks.

A half-hour later, I walked into the room where the elders' council would be held and sat down, empty. Even now, minutes before the story-telling would begin, I believed I had no story to tell. I also believed I was the only one whose time in the wilderness had been a waste. How would I tell them, these 18 people who had become dear friends? I didn't know. It would be short, whatever I said. Short, but not sweet. A quick admission of defeat. No vision. No life purpose discovered. No words of wisdom from tree or rock or lizard. Nothing.

And then, without warning, without the slightest preceding breath of hope, something came to me. It was a realization about shadow, and yet, paradoxically, it

allowed one ray of light to burst through a tiny crack in
my unconsciousness. I reached for my journal and
hurriedly scrawled a few words. A moment later, I wrote
something else. Soon I was scribbling furiously; realizations crowded into my mind and tumbled onto the page,
one on the heels of another, barely a breath in between,
just as the "Why?s" of my lament had flowed faster and
faster from my lips that morning in the wilderness before
I'd lost my heart. And this was the first I knew -- the
first I'd ever imagined, in fact -- that the Voice might live
somewhere beyond The Canyon. That the Voice,
amazingly enough, might be with me still.

Here, then, is the story of the gifts the Voice
brought -- realizations that swept away the crushing
burden I had carried since the last afternoon of my solo;
realizations that let me know with relief beyond words
that I did, in fact, have a story to tell, and that the quest
had not, after all, been a waste; realizations that exposed
possible meaning behind the apparent meaninglessness
of events and thoughts and landscape:

Shadow had been a persistent companion during
the three days and nights of my solo experience. My solo
spot faced north, and consequently was shaded for much
of the day. Suddenly, I saw symbolism in the shadow that
had chilled me, and my heart opened as if to an old
friend. Far from being an accidental consequence of my
poor sense of direction, my heavily shaded power spot
now revealed itself as a metaphor for my whole experience, which had thrust me, kicking and screaming, into
the figurative/Jungian "shadow" of my psyche -- that
dark place where I'd stuffed the emotions, the feelings,
the traits that I'd deemed unacceptable. In other words,
the shadow of the canyon walls had been trying to tell

me something. I simply hadn't understood the language.
Also, I'd ended up rejecting my solo spot.
Especially after my encounter with Fear on the afternoon
of the hives, I had grown alienated from the sacred spot
that I'd chosen as shelter and teacher. I could no longer
see its beauty; my spot no longer felt safe; I no longer felt
I belonged there. Fear did what it does best -- cut me off
from the world around me, and from the world deep
inside, as well. And so, on the day the group hiked out, I
had felt absolutely no connection to this supposedly
sacred land, except for the emotional charge that was my
desire to leave it. This rejection, too, I now recognized as
metaphor: I had rejected my spot just like I'd historically
rejected my own shadow, preferring to believe only in the
"nice" parts of myself and thereby denying half of my
being and half of what it meant to be human.

The shame I'd associated with my recent bout of
fear, anger and negativity was symbolic, too: symbolic of
the larger shame I associated with having a "dark side."
I rejected my dark side, and so I rejected myself, and so I
expected others to reject me too. Acting on this certainty
of rejection, I had on our last day in The Canyon dis-
tanced myself from the very people most likely to support
me. In rejecting my dark side, I also cut myself off from
the natural world. It takes a whole person to communi-
cate with the universe; I'd denied the wholeness of my
being. And so I'd felt weak and frightened and alone.

Furthermore, in denying my dark side I'd inadvertently given it power. That's how anger and exhaustion
led me to kick apart our stone pile and leave the rocks
where they lay; how fear came to guide my steps on the
long hike out; how I came to care so little about crushing
the crypto. That, too, was symbolic. For as long as I could
remember, I had judged harshly anyone who harmed the
Earth, hating what I believed to be their stupidity and

their greed. I'd felt no connection to these destroyers; they might as well have been aliens from some dark and distant planet. Yet suddenly I saw that we were of the same species, after all, these destroyers and I; they, too, had given their dark sides power. They, too, had let fear be their guide. And fear, seeing only itself, would be better off blind. In my case, I'd been afraid of not making it out of The Canyon. The destroyers, too, were afraid -- afraid of not having enough; afraid of that which they didn't understand. Strange as it seemed, I knew in that moment that some of the richest men in the world were also the most afraid; and that fear fueled their lust for the riches of the Earth, for money and power without measure. Fear, rational or not, is fear just the same. And this one cliché is true: Fear, not people, is the enemy.

So it came to me, my Vision. Sitting on the floor, surrounded by 18 people and their animated conversations, I heard only the Voice -- the Voice of Soul, the Voice of Great Spirit, the Voice of the Earth, they all spoke in unison and told me the truth, a truth so basic almost everyone had forgotten it, but nonetheless, the Truth. And this is what they said:

"You're human, and to be human is to harbor both light and dark. Your challenge is to face your shadow, to learn to acknowledge and accept it. Shine the light of love on the dark qualities of your own humanity; only then can they be transformed; only then will the darkness lose power over you.

"Accept and love all parts of yourself. Only then can you become who you truly are. Only then can you discover and fulfill your life's purpose. Only then will the trees and the rocks and the lizards talk back."

Loving oneself -- now *that* is powerful medicine. My Soul and the Earth had conspired to save me; they prescribed the perfect healing dose.

Chapter 20

> " 'Look at your face,' she said, 'you have surren-
> dered your masks.' I went alone to my room, lit a
> candle, and looked into the mirror. I was trans-
> formed. I saw the eyes, the face, the spirit, the
> soul, the healer, the student, the teacher, the
> ancient one, the child, and the Beast. They were
> all me."
>
> -- Jeri, in *Woman Who Glows in the Dark* by
> Elena Avila with Joy Parker

A few hours later. I sat in the circle, this time not
alone, my heart open, feelings of gratitude washing over
and through me. In recognizing my connection to something so much larger than myself -- for I knew, beyond a
shadow of a doubt, that nothing on the quest had been
an accident; that I had been the oft-unknowing recipient
of an unending series of gifts from the Voice, from the
Earth, from Spirit -- I had been born anew. I'd discovered, deep within, a direct connection to Spirit; it goes by
the name of Soul. And Soul reminded me that I'd come to
Earth with a purpose. I might not know that purpose
consciously, but my Soul knew. And through listening to
the Voice, through having the courage to walk through
shadows, I would come to know it too. The Earth -- a
very powerful ally -- had conspired to help me. I realized,

also, that I was not unique; we'd all come here with a purpose, and part of all of our journeys was remembering. Re-membering. Putting back together our lives; reconnecting our personas with our Soul and with Spirit; rebalancing dark and light. I am never alone on my journey; nor are you. I am loved; so are you. And just like in The Canyon, there are no accidents. . . well, hardly any, anyway.

Soaking up these realizations as I'd longed to soak up sunlight in The Canyon, I felt at home in myself as never before. I was, however briefly, comfortable with all parts of myself -- even those I scarcely knew, even those that dwelled in shadow. I also felt very much at home with this group of 18 brave and magical beings who had, in fact, slain dragons. Dragons of fear, of illusion, of ignorance. My heart was open; so were theirs. In that place of the heart, we spoke without speaking.

Later, during a break when people rose from their places on the floor -- some stiffly, muscles aching, legs and backs remembering 35-pound packs -- to wander off for tea or fresh air or that luxury called indoor plumbing, two people approached me, separately -- one a fellow quester, one an apprentice guide. Both told me that I looked like a different person from the one who'd begun the quest. That my face had opened, softened.

"*I look in the mirror and see kinder eyes,*" I wrote in my journal. "*Direct, prolonged eye contact -- easy for me generally -- is even easier now.*" What I didn't write but what was true nonetheless was that I looked younger, far less serious, "fresher," as if I'd just arisen from a deep sleep of magical Earth dreams and was, for perhaps the first time in my life, 100% awake.

Chapter 21

> *"We returned to our places, these kingdoms, no longer at ease here, in the old dispensation, with an alien people clutching their gods."*
>
> -- T.S. Eliot, "Journey of the Magi"

The next day. The quest ended, abruptly or so it seemed. One last circle, lingering looks into each other's eyes, long embraces. A challenge to go home and share our visions with our people, whatever that might mean. Then, for the second time in less than a week, each quester shouldered a pack and walked resolutely off, alone. For me, there was no time for long good-byes; my flight was scheduled to depart in 45 minutes from an airport 20 minutes away. Now, an hour or so later, I sat in the front aisle seat of a small plane headed from Durango to Denver, beside Mary, the oldest quester, the one whose presence and perseverance had inspired me to put one foot in front of the other in defiance of my doubts and fear and pain. We were glad for each other's company, both suspended in an indefinable place between there and here, between the world of dreams and the one called "reality". Crossing the mountains, the plane suddenly dropped and pitched; by the time it stabilized, my stomach was in my throat and Mary's soda, on the floor. The flight attendant smiled, clutching at a seat back to keep her balance -- "it's always rough here." And I, the one whose face had opened into full wakefulness, I realized for perhaps the first time in my life that it was all OK -- everything was OK. Even if the plane crashed, everything would be OK. Not that I wanted to die, especially not now. But if I did, it would be OK. I felt an extraordinary sense of peace. Everything was OK.

And then we arrived in Denver.

A woman with suspicious face (myself before the quest, times three) told me to step aside and open my daypack (not to be confused with the backpack, which had been checked in Durango and, though I didn't know it yet, was already "lost," destined to fly home not with me but on a later flight, the tarpaulin tied to it vanishing mysteriously somewhere along the way). "Sure," I said, puzzled. This was a first; never before had I been singled out by airport security to have my belongings searched. What, I wondered, did this woman suspect?

Whatever it was, she was wrong. And I suddenly remembered a strange descriptor our guide had used for our group of returning questers: "poison to society." He'd meant it as a compliment. I figured he'd been referring to the fact that we'd changed. That we'd be seeing the world with clearer vision. That we'd question things. That we might even throw out our television sets, as he had urged, TV being one of culture's most potent tools for limiting our dreams. That we'd strive to be true to ourselves. That we'd strive to manifest our Soul's purpose -- even if doing so meant defying some of the rules and beliefs that society held dear. Is that what the woman had seen in my face? "Poison"? Something unfamiliar, which she didn't understand, and something that therefore scared her?

Vindicated and ready to laugh out loud at the incongruous image of my 5-foot-3, 120-pound self as someone to be wary of, I grabbed my pack and hurried out into the main concourse. And there was where it became brutally clear that everything was not, in fact, OK. Everywhere was noise and movement and jarring images; stimuli piled upon stimuli crashing up against yet more stimuli, all demanding my attention, my money, and especially, my life. Everyone was rushing, pushing, scowling. No one seemed at peace. Judging from the conversations I overheard, peace was barely a blip on the radar screen of the travelers' collective unconscious. If this is society, I thought, I can think of nothing better to be than poison.

Long minutes of standing in a long line of impatient passengers later, I wrote this in my journal: "*Sandwiched between two people in a middle, was-to-be window seat on the plane back to Newark. Feeling on the verge of tears. Not prepared for how difficult leaving Colorado would be. . . . If I lean back in my seat, I see Batman and Robin* (the movie, not a hallucination). *Very disconcerting. Look out the window.*

"*Woman next to me just said, 'Sad about John Denver, isn't it?' Apparently he died yesterday in a small-plane crash. Another world. . .*"

And in a long list of impressions not yet recorded, a cushion between myself and the cramped cabin in which I sat, elbows pressed close to a body whose memory of confined spaces had been all but obliterated: "*AMAZING! Yesterday morning, walking into elders' council with not a clue as to what I would say. Having connection after connection click for me . . .ending up marveling deeply at how I did, in fact, get not what I wanted on the quest but what I needed. (For example, connecting my 'rejection' of my power spot with its being*

79

in the shadow, and cold -- that is, rejecting my own
shadow, including the parts of me that I perceive as cold).
    "More connections made the day of elders' council:
that on the day we hiked out, I was in a place of dark-
ness, alienation and fear -- & I didn't tell anyone because
I was ashamed. Until I truly embrace my shadow, noth-
ing else will happen (e.g., I won't hear the trees talking
back). . . . Our guide noted that the universe arranged to
have me face my own deepest fears (death?), via the hives
-- and, I added, via my fear of falling, body torn apart by
the not-quite-blood-red rocks."

    And, I came to understand later, it made me face
what was probably my greatest fear of all: the fear that I
was not likable, that I was not lovable, that I was cold,
that the qualities in my shadow were not part of me, but
instead that they defined me. That I was my shadow . . .
And that my shadow was very bad indeed.

Chapter 22

> *". . . we're beginning to glimpse an alternative
> kind of experience . . . moments in our lives that
> feel different somehow, more intense and inspir-
> ing. But we don't know what this experience is or
> how to make it last, and when it ends we're left
> feeling dissatisfied and restless with a life that
> seems ordinary again."*
>
> -- James Redfield, *The Celestine Prophecy*

First day 'home' (Oct. 14): With great difficulty,
my words halting and my mind far away, I told my partner the story of the quest. I tried to do so in a sacred
way, and so I lit candles. I tried to be fully present, and
so I stared deep into my partner's eyes, hoping to anchor
myself there in that moment, that room, that chair. I
hoped, too, that my eyes would tell the truth that words
could not, that they would paint pictures of the desert
canyons and evoke feelings that refused to be named.
But no matter how many candles burned or how many
words I tried or how intent my stare, I was miserably
aware that I was failing: failing to stay present, my mind
wandering and my body and spirit sluggish with the
accumulated fatigue of more than a week of adrenaline,
exhilaration, desperation and epiphany; and failing, by a

long shot, to do justice to the story I tried to tell. Finally, I simply stopped -- a storyteller run down like a clock that stops ticking, the story fading, no happy ending . . . in fact, no ending at all.

And having stopped, I felt empty. And the emptiness frightened me, as if, in the attempted telling, my story -- life-changer, gift, barely opened book -- had somehow left me. And the idea of my story's leaving me -- vanishing like the shooting stars that had lit the Utah sky for one brief and beautiful moment, a moment passing so quickly that my belief in them was sorely tested -- was unbearable.

Slowly, I got up and walked to the laundry room where my pack lay, sides bulging, and emptied as many of its contents as possible directly into the washing machine. The rest I piled on the floor. Then I loaded the empty pack into my car and drove to the shopping mall where I'd rented it. The mall. A brutal place, for one so recently at home in a remote southwestern canyon. In my struggle to hold on -- to myself, my experience, my soul -- I sought affirming signs from the universe, and found one in the small miracle of a parking space just outside the mall entrance closest to the store where I'd rented the pack -- the normally elusive "perfect space."

On the way home, I found another when I stopped at a bookstore to buy my first book on shadow, those disowned parts of oneself that live on despite ego's efforts to deny them. Written by the Jungian analyst Robert Johnson, it was called *Owning Your Own Shadow* and was short enough to feel deceptively inconsequential. I opened my wallet and found a small amount of change -- the exact change for the book. I left smiling.

Five days post-quest (Oct. 18). "Realized the other day that one reason I no doubt 'rejected' my solo spot in

*The Canyon was because it represented the rage I felt on
the morning of breaking camp. Rage is an emotion I'd
learned to be ashamed of; in rejecting my rage, I also
rejected the place on the Earth where I'd experienced it.
Guilt by association . . . Confusing -- how DO I
love/honor my shadow, without giving it any power? How
do I stop denying the parts of myself that I and others
have considered shameful, without having them act out,
assert themselves, 'take over' ?"*

Six days P-Q (Oct. 19). On our property sat a grove
of evergreens that I called "the forest." It wasn't, exactly;
there was no diversity of understory plants, no shrubs or
ferns beneath the trees, and many of the evergreens were
so close it appeared they'd been planted as Christmas
trees, then allowed through some benevolent twist of fate
to simply be evergreens -- growing fat and tall, often
asymmetrical, dead branches amidst the live, home to
chattering squirrels and birds. This gathering of trees
was but a dim shadow of the woodlands that once teemed
with life of nearly unimaginable diversity, woodlands
that had blanketed the East before the coming of
Europeans, the white men who took not only the forest's
name ("Penn's Woods") but also virtually all its trees. But
to me, the forest on our property was a breath of wild-
ness, a place where humans virtually never trod, the
exceptions being my partner's grandson and myself, he
treasuring it for what it was and I, as much for what it
wasn't.

Within this forest grew one particular tree that I'd
been drawn to from the first time I saw it -- a magnifi-
cent towering tree with gracefully drooping boughs and
"needles" that were soft and delicate, its new growth a
vibrant green. More than once, through some mechanism
as magical as it was inexplicable, this tree's presence had

unlocked feelings previously stuck deep inside. Once, I'd leaned my head against its trunk and cried.

On this day, I sat beneath Tree on my Therma Lounger camp chair, the chair that had been my nearly constant companion on the quest, cushion between me and the desert's hard-packed earth and rocks. With me were my journal and the photos of Utah I'd just picked up -- pictures taken quickly, with little thought and a recyclable panoramic camera that I'd purchased as a sorry compromise, my 35-mm camera and lenses too heavy for a backpack and, just as important, too seductive to one whose major purpose in trekking to the canyons was deepening her connection to soul, not addictively pursuing the perfect picture. *"Thought I might cry when I saw them,"* I wrote of the photographs. *"But, in fact, the pictures are like the words I've used to try to describe my experience -- sadly inadequate. No tears."*

I leaned back in my chair and breathed in greedily the scents of dampness, pine and decaying wood. Then I wrote about the trip to the city to pick up the pictures: *"I ended up feeling shell-shocked. So many people, so many cars, so many THINGS. . ."*

Another name for this shell-shocked feeling was "not belonging." For weeks after the quest, it turned out, I felt like a stranger to my own life. Coming home from the vision quest was like awakening one morning to find that most of my clothing no longer fit, and the only way to find the skirts and pants and shirts that did was to try them all on, painstaking piece by piece. This sense of not belonging left me off-balance, prone to feeling sad and empty and dull. And while the hard edge of strangeness eventually dulled too, never again did I feel that I truly belonged in this place where bulldozers swarmed across the land, leaving behind strip malls, warehouses and ugly soul-less over-priced houses where once had been trees and meadows and farms.

Even more significantly, perhaps, I never again felt that I truly belonged to the culture that had shaped me, scouring me as it had scoured the Earth. One meaning of "belonging" is "owned by", as in, "that house, that car, that (fill in the blank) is mine!" I never again felt that I was owned by a culture whose values were not my own, a culture driven by the pursuit of stuff and speed and supposed superiority over the natural world on which our very lives depend. And so, I started questioning everything; I haven't stopped since. Perhaps our guide was right; perhaps I really am poison.

At that moment, though, I wasn't so much questioning as holding on, hoping for clearer vision. "*Had a dream last night related to the vision quest*," I wrote in my journal. "*Awoke 'hearing' these sentences, as if I'd tuned in to a frequency normally accessible only to my dreaming self: 'Are you taken care of?' ' No, but I will be.' A clear message that the gifts from my quest will keep unfolding. I think again of Eagle (my 'guide' to the west, a power animal whose image came to me during a session of guided imagery preceding my three-day solo), when I asked what I could do to ensure that I'd find what I was seeking. Eagle spoke just one word -- BELIEVE.*"

Yet already -- a mere eight days separating me from the canyons -- my ability to believe was fading in the same way that the canyon dust was disappearing from the hiking boots I wore as I trudged through high wet grass back to the house.

Chapter 23

> *"Ignoring the gold can be as damaging as ignor-*
> *ing the dark side of the psyche, and some people*
> *may suffer a severe shock or illness before they*
> *learn how to let the gold out."*
>
> -- Robert Johnson, *Owning Your Own Shadow*

9 days P-Q (Oct. 22). On this day, my journal writing was like a choppy lake is to a canoeist -- it bounced me about from one day to the next, from a waking dream to a sleeping one.

First, I wrote about having taken my golden retriever for a walk on the Appalachian Trail the day before. Not surprisingly, I'd felt more 'at home' there than anywhere else since I'd been home from the quest, with the exception, of course, of the forest.

Then I wrote about an idea that had come to me a day or so earlier, while my partner and I, a two-person consulting team, prepared for a training for the staff of a non-profit agency about evaluating the effectiveness of their work. Inside me, a great resistance had begun to build; I could barely force myself to think within the boundaries drawn by an evaluator's eye, even though the view was a fairly expansive one and the work itself, interesting and useful. "*It struck me that I 'have to' and will make additional changes,*" I wrote in my journal. "*I have to bring my work closer to my heart. The quest wasn't just a dream. . ."* In other words, fine as the work was, it wasn't really mine. To do something else, to do something that was mine, my real work, the work of my soul -- that was a waking dream of the highest order.

Finally, I wrote about my nighttime dreams -- or, more accurately, about how little of them I'd been remembering. What I did remember was a fragment of a dream involving William, a figure from my past whom I hadn't seen for years or thought of in nearly as long, a figure who, perhaps more than anyone else I'd known personally, represented darkness. In the dream, I was talking with him yet feeling uneasy -- *"feeling that I couldn't really trust him, beyond a superficial point . . ."*

----

12 days P-Q (Oct. 25). William. Why would I trust him? In waking life, he had betrayed me in a singularly malicious way -- a way that required planning, and cunning, and a willingness to lie with the fervor of a missionary. His appearance in my dream the other night had been, among other things, a demonstration of how limited was my early understanding of shadow; for in dreaming of William, I dreamt of darkness. And darkness and shadow are not, I repeat are not, the same.

"It is also astonishing," wrote Robert Johnson in his deceptively skinny book, *"that some very good characteristics turn up in the shadow. Generally, the ordinary, mundane characteristics are the norm. Anything less than this goes into shadow. But anything better also goes into the shadow! Some of the pure gold of our personality is relegated to the shadow because it can find no place in that great leveling process that is culture."*

In other words, our culture and our families teach us that only certain qualities and behaviors are acceptable; the rest, be they signs of weakness or marks of greatness, are repressed into shadow. That's how shad-

ow grows fat from not just the darkness in our
personalities, but also some of our most brilliant light!

The concept of gold in the shadow was entirely
new to me when I read it, so new that it was like the
raindrops beading on my jacket during a cloudburst in
the canyons -- making contact, but failing to penetrate. I
read the words, but they didn't sink in. My jacket had
been waterproof; my mind, like most people's, repelled
ideas that challenged accustomed ways of thinking.
Repelling this particular idea wouldn't have surprised
Johnson: "*Curiously, people resist the noble aspects of
their shadow more strenuously than they hide the dark
sides. To draw the skeletons out of the closet is relatively
easy, but to own the gold in the shadow is terrifying. It is
more disrupting to find that you have a profound nobility
of character than to find out you are a bum. Of course you
are both; but one does not discover these two elements at
the same time. The gold is related to our higher calling,
and this can be hard to accept at certain stages of life. . .*"

Apparently, this was not the time for me to realize
my higher calling. Instead, I focused on another concept
I'd read in Johnson's book: paradox. In essence, he urged
readers to expand their minds to make room for seeming
opposites. I liked that idea, perhaps because my own life
had come to feel like a continuous clash of opposites -- on
the one side, the me who had quested, an extraordinary
act that changed everything; on the other, the me who
was squeezing herself back into an ordinary life, a life in
which nothing, it seemed, had changed.

Here's a paradox, I thought much later: The person in my past who represents darkness, AND the person
in my present who represents the loving wisdom of a
vision quest guide, are both named William! Oh, that
universe -- what a sense of humor!

Chapter 24

> *"It is this vulnerability, this nakedness, that
> enables us to bring up our shadow -- the
> anxieties, fears, and pain which we often hide
> from ourselves and others."*
>
> -- Marcia Starck and Gynne Stern, *The Dark
> Goddess: Dancing with the Shadow*

*1*7 *days P-Q (Oct. 30).* More realizations, recorded
in my journal: "*Just as our guides had hoped, my ego
WAS defeated on the quest. I realize the all-night vigil
played a major role in ego's defeat. It transported me
beyond tired, to a stark place of raw feeling, a place where
the usual interval between emotion and expression was
greatly compressed -- obliterated, even -- leaving no room
for the censoring effect of the ego. If my ego hadn't been
defeated -- if my 'rational' mind hadn't acquiesced to the
irrational -- I never would have been so angry and fed up
and negative on the morning of my return to base camp.
Nor would I have been so brutally conscious of the depth
of my fear before and during our ascent from the canyons.
Normally, ego is a double agent -- feeding fear with its
addictions to control, to 'security', to 'safety' (the thought
of losing any one of them unbearable, and therefore scary
as hell!); but also 'protecting' me from fear with its*

formidable denial. Yet that morning and afternoon, ego's defenses were down. And so the fear crashed into me like a runaway train. There was no cushion of denial to blunt the pain, just as there had been no cushion of civility to lighten my black mood that morning. In other words, it was through the temporary defeat of ego that I felt -- and for a time, but only for a time, became -- the dark side of my shadow."

Chapter 25

> "Sometimes dreams are wiser than waking."
>
> -- Black Elk, as reported by John G. Neihardt in
> *Black Elk Speaks*

*1*8 days P-Q (Halloween). "Dreamt last night that
*I was gazing out the living room window when I noticed
the gray tail feathers of a bird -- looked closer and saw
that it was a very scraggly, mangy-looking hawk. I
assumed it had recently caught and eaten a songbird; the
area around the hawk looked really mangy, too, the
ground littered with what I assume were flesh and
feathers. While I watched, this scruffy-looking hawk
began to transform -- it 'came into its own', becoming who
it really was -- a being both earthy and majestic. It
straightened up, fluffed up its feathers, and looked at me
with eyes that were bright and keen and healthy. And
then, to my wonderment, this chameleon-hawk transformed once more, this time into a beautiful stone version
of itself -- a natural 'sculpture' standing tall, peering out
over mountains and valley."*

I awoke to the refreshing awareness of the power
in that dream. And I found myself wondering whether
hawk's meal of the songbird had been more than it first
seemed -- a meal, yes, but perhaps also a metaphor, a

metaphor for taking in parts of one's own self, and in doing so becoming whole. A metaphor for having the voice needed to sing one's own song -- all of the notes, not just the melodious ones -- and thereby growing grounded, solid and strong as stone.

Metaphor, after all, is the language of dreams. In my dream, that hawk had been hungry, and in eating was transformed. I was hungry, too -- for purpose, for clarity, for wholeness. Was the dream telling me that I needed to figuratively "eat" my own shadow in order to be made whole? To take in and "own" all the disowned parts of myself, in order to be transformed? If so, I thought, frowning slightly at the memory of my first sight of the hawk and the littered ground around him, I'd better get accustomed to the mess!

And what of the hawk's having turned finally to stone? In the Bible, turning to stone is punishment. But nothing about the dream felt negative or frightening or punitive. On the contrary, it felt hopeful. Stone is solid. Stone is dependable. And in this case, the stone was right outside the living room window -- there for me to see, anytime I chose to look.

The stone was right outside the "window" -- a gift for me, anytime I chose to close my eyes and see.

----

19 days P-Q (Nov. 1). More dreams. But the one I recalled with the greatest clarity was only a fragment of a dream: I'd left the lights on in my car, and the battery was dead. "*I need / want to conceive some ceremony in honor of this dream,*" I wrote, remembering a lesson from the quest. That lesson: Dreams are gifts, and enacting a ceremony based on a dream is a way to acknowledge the gift. In dreams, something other than our rational mind -- call it the subconscious, call it the "higher self", call it the Voice -- speaks to us in symbols. By enacting a cere-

mony, we respond in the same language; we enter into a
dialogue with the part of ourselves that's sending us a
message. In effect, we say, "I got it!" And depending on
the message, we may want to do much more than that; in
this case, a battery recharge definitely seemed in order.

----

2 days later, 21 days P-Q (Nov. 3). I entered the
forest, carrying my chair, a bottle of water, my journal,
and a sense of the sacredness of my dreams, both nighttime and waking. I had had little experience in the
creation of ceremony, but I was becoming fluent in the
language of symbol and metaphor. That's what happens
when you become aware of the Voice; you listen for It
everywhere, and you find It in the events of your life, the
patterns of the clouds, the content of your dreams. The
symbolism in the dead-battery dream was so sharp it
nearly cut me, and what it told me was this: I was tired,
run down, in need of a "recharge."

And so I stood, feet planted securely on
Grandmother Earth, both arms extending above my
head, each hand holding on to a bough of Tree, breathing
deeply, envisioning the Earth's energy coursing up
through my feet and out through my hands into Tree,
and from Tree back down to the Earth again, and from
the Earth back into me. An unbroken circle of energy and
love. Then, I crouched down on the damp-smelling
ground with its brittle cushion of needles and drank
water, deeply -- water, symbolic of the energy, the
vitality, the life-giving generosity of Grandmother Earth.
Water, literal life-giver, not just in the desert but here,
there, wherever you sit as you read this book. Water, a
few drops of which I returned to the Earth, symbol of my
deep gratitude for the land and the life that sustain me.
Next, I stood by Tree, resting my head gently on its
trunk, laying a hand on each side, saying a silent thank

Earth Dreams

you, allowing my gratefulness to ride the gentle waves of
energy emanating from my body. Finally, I crouched
down once again and put both hands palm-down and flat
upon the Earth, energy flowing both ways. And the
ceremony was done.

"*Feeling in awe and great appreciation. Feeling at
peace, clear and -- yes! -- recharged. Even sitting here on
my Therma Lounger, I visualize the energy flowing
through my feet and on into the rest of my body. Thank
you, Great Spirit, Grandmother Earth! I feel that Tree
reawakened the canyon consciousness inside of me. It is
an amazing, incredible blessing to know that
Grandmother is always here, ready to love and nourish
me.*"

I went on to record a passing thought: "*It occurred
to me the other day that perhaps I am to write about
shadow. Hard to find books on shadow; and it seems to
me that the denial of shadow may be responsible for most
of what's wrong in the world today. Somewhere in the
trees around me, Crow laughs.*"

And finally, I wrote this:"*A dream from last night:
Bill has suggested I do another quest -- a special quest --
perhaps the whole quest as a solo . . .* " I did not yet
realize the reality in the dream. Did not yet comprehend
that the quest was continuing -- accelerating, even -- and
that it was now up to me to be both seeker and guide.
Instead, I remained sitting, head tilted back, listening to
the chattering of birds and watching their shadowy forms
dart among the branches.

Chapter 26

> "There are no clear and final answers, there are
> only discussions and thoughts and silent wonder
> filling each moment."
>
> -- Brian Andreas, "Strange Dreams"

30 days P-Q (Nov. 12). On this day, a day when
agitation drove me into the cold steel arms of the
NordicTrack, I tried to stop thinking. I wanted to simply
be -- to ski my way into a state of mindful mindlessness,
to feel my muscles (even when they hurt), to feel my
breath (even when it ripped in and out in ragged gasps),
to feel my place on this Earth (even here in the basement), and not -- above all, not -- to think. Not to worry.
Not to analyze. Not to rationalize. Not to whip myself
with my own expectations, not to beat myself with my
own harsh judgments, not to make myself sad with my
own regrets. Instead, to simply breathe, and ski, and be.

And in the midst of my breathing-skiing-being,
two realizations slipped into my mind, occupying a space
normally jammed tight with mindless "chatter," junk
mail to oneself -- a space opened up by the sheer power of
my will to be released, however temporarily, from the
tyranny of thoughtless thoughts.

The first realization had to do with the message

Earth Dreams

I'd received during guided imagery more than a month earlier -- the message that my power spot would be somewhere that I could fly to. I'd interpreted that message to mean my spot would be easily accessible -- an effortless climb -- and it had been. Now, however, I realized a potential meaning far more profound, a potential meaning that was meaningful now: That I could "fly" to my power spot anytime, in my mind and heart; that I didn't have to travel to Utah to be transformed. At that, I smiled and skied a little faster.

The second realization struck me as so obvious that I almost stumbled off the machine in my amazement and amusement; how could it possibly have taken me more than a month to see?!? Overlooking my power spot had been a rock that looked like an eagle; I called it, naturally, Eagle Rock. Yet not once during my solo or the four weeks hence had I made the obvious connection between this rock and Eagle the power animal / guide who'd come to me in a vision and challenged me to "Believe." Later that day, I wrote in my journal, "*Only now do I see how Eagle was watching over me! And again, I hear Eagle's message: 'Believe.' I felt it, with all of my being -- an awareness of being so loved, so guided.*"

Felt it so strongly that, instead of falling off the machine, I regained my rhythm and skied, elated and grateful, for a half-mile more than usual.

Chapter 27

> *"Whether you believe you can do a thing or not,*
> *you are right."*
>
> -- Henry Ford

3 days later, 33 days P-Q (Nov. 15). "*Awoke in the middle of the night last night, immediately after a dream that felt very significant. Considered forcing myself fully awake in order to write it down, but was sure I'd remember it in the morning. And I do, but only the second part:*

"*I walk through a 'doorway' ('real' or figurative, I'm not sure) into a scene from World War II. As I do, I am amazed -- in awe -- because I immediately know that this scene has manifested solely (or soul-ly??) to teach me something -- it is here for me. I know that it isn't 'real' in an everyday, earth-plane kind of way; in other words, I know on a deep level that I am safe. I walk confidently between two lines of soldiers. Most appear relaxed, yet the tension is palpable and everyone seems to be waiting for something. Projectiles that resemble large cannon balls are being fired over the crest of a hill, although I can't see who's shooting them. Now I realize that cannon balls are also being fired at us -- one is hurtling through the air, headed directly toward the spot where I stand. I cringe, trying to get as low to the ground as possible. I wait -- for the explosion, the carnage, the pain. I am aware that I will have to see lots of suffering and gore -- but it doesn't come. I am crazy, waiting . . . (then I wake up).*

"*It strikes me that in that dream, I am simultaneously petrified by fear AND totally confident in my safety. What a powerful metaphor for life on this earth plane!*"

Walking between two lines of soldiers -- between shadow and consciousness, perhaps? Or, more likely, this "war" represented the conflict between my ego and my shadow -- both sides hurling explosives at the other, yet nothing blowing up. Certainly my ego viewed my shadow parts as the enemy; after all, ego had sent some of them into hiding; and for those shamed into shadow before the formation of my ego, ego worked hard to keep them there. Ego had heard and internalized the judgments of others; ego had sought acceptance and approval above all else; ego had tried to please by stuffing full what poet Robert Bly calls "the long bag we drag behind us" - a.k.a. our shadow. And so it was natural that ego would do almost anything to keep my shadow from the light. But what about my shadow parts? Would they in turn wage a war on ego? In a way, yes. The parts of myself that had been stuffed into shadow posed a grave threat to ego in that they challenged its denial; they said, in effect, "We are here! You, ego, are not the totality of this human being; she is more than you, she is all of us too."

The ego, of course, seldom gives in gracefully. Perhaps a round of "explosives" is exactly what's needed to burst through its denial. Significantly, the cannonball in the dream didn't actually hurt me.

As for the experience of seeing or feeling suffering, life on Earth is full of it. But sometimes, what is most crippling of all is the anticipation. The waiting, sometimes for suffering that never comes. And yet if the waiting means being immobilized by fear -- if the anticipation itself evokes negative images and gut-tightness, hard-heartedness and pain -- then it is suffering. Insidious suffering, standing like an unyielding wall between us and our dreams.

I knew all about that kind of suffering, for in my shadow lived a part of me -- I think of her now as the scared little girl -- who expected the worst. That shadow part of myself was forever worrying about bad things that might happen, and though virtually none of them ever did, the anticipation itself was crippling. At this point in my life, I was beginning to realize how costly it was to live in a prison of my own fear's making. The first step toward getting free, paradoxical as it may sound, was acknowledging that scared little girl inside myself, and loving her. If I were to live out my life's purpose, I'd definitely need her help.

Later, I wrote this in my journal: "*Have a strong sense or desire that what I'd like to do -- what would be 'right' -- would be to do my writing and soul work as first priority, and to fit our other work in around it, not vice versa like it is now.*"

Another passing thought. Given its similarity to the one recorded 12 days earlier ("*. . .perhaps I am to write about shadow. . .*"), it did indicate, at the least, that these thoughts were passing by more often.

Chapter 28

> *"We need to reintegrate all parts of us, even the parts that seem wild, scary, dirty, and unattractive, back into the whole. Unless we can do this, we will never really have the ability to live up to our true capacity, and to experience our fullest capacity for love."*
>
> -- Elena Avila with Joy Parker, *Woman Who Glows in the Dark*

36 days P-Q (Nov. 18). The night before, I'd been together again with my fellow questers -- this time in dreamtime, yet the lessons were no less real. I'd been talking earnestly to a quester named Lisa (very positive, evoking the "gold" in the shadow), telling her how much I wished we could get together (how much I yearned to reconnect with the light in my shadow?). But she was half-asleep and didn't respond (uh oh). Then, while everyone else left for a cafeteria (food, a.k.a. nurturing), I stayed behind. Bill, our guide (the wise inner guide who lives inside me?) joined me, as did an aggressive, menacing, angry wasp who flew around us, diving toward us and then away. Bill told me to kill it; he's allergic, and I knew that a single sting could kill him. But the only "weapon" I had was a cafeteria tray. *"I am aware that the*

*wasp is dangerous, so I have to be careful; I try to be very
alert, and quick on my feet."* I swung the cafeteria tray,
ineffectually. *"I am not aggressive enough -- or perhaps
it's that I can't stretch far enough."* (hmm. . . stretching.
What in my life do I need to stretch toward? What has
felt like "too much of a stretch?")

Then, in the midst of my unsuccessful, "wussy"
even, attempts to kill the wasp, I looked over and saw
William. William, the one from my past, the one who represented the darkest parts of shadow. *"I know he will
come and help me. I am actually glad to see him; his
presence gives me comfort."* But a moment later -- before
William moved from the periphery of my vision -- the
wasp sat down and I hit it. Not very hard, yet it stayed
there and I hit it once again. Though neither blow
seemed strong enough to kill it, the wasp's color began to
change. It grew darker (!?), and I wondered if I had killed
it after all. It also changed shape; what once had been a
wasp looked now like a gargoyle -- mouse-like body, but
with wings. Hitting the creature left me feeling sick, but
most upsetting of all was seeing it grow darker.

Well. That was a dream that felt full of meaning --
overripe, even, a tomato bursting on the vine. I wasn't
sure I got it all; am not sure I get it still. But I did have
three major insights: *"Shadow could / can be my ally!"*
Even the parts I associate with darkness, parts like
aggressiveness and the potential to do violence. *"I was
relieved to see William; he helped me feel safe, because I
knew he would help me."* Of course William didn't
actually help me kill the wasp-turned-gargoyle, but the
realization that he could have may have made my own
aim truer. Perhaps when we acknowledge that within us
lies the capacity for extreme action, we have the confi-
dence not to use it. Perhaps when we acknowledge that
we are not, in fact, a "wuss," we are able to claim our

true power -- not power over others, but the power that arises within.

The second insight was a simple one: "*Using aggression against the darkness can backfire.*" In other words -- words we've all heard -- violence does breed violence, and hatred, hatred. When struck, the menacing wasp grew uglier and darker. Would there have been a better way to "protect" Bill? A more loving and gentle way?

The final insight was this: "*If there are male and female aspects of the self -- which there are, regardless of one's gender -- then it follows that there are also male and female aspects of shadow. In the dream, the female aspect of my shadow was asleep; the male aspect was awake, and prepared to 'rescue' me. . .*"

Chapter 29

> *"It is wrong, then, to chide the novel for being*
> *fascinated by mysterious coincidences . . . but it*
> *is right to chide man for being blind to such*
> *coincidences in his daily life. For he thereby*
> *deprives his life of a dimension of beauty."*
>
> -- Milan Kundera, *The Unbearable Lightness of*
> *Being*

2 *days later, 38 days post-quest (Nov. 20)*. I awoke
feeling irritable, and so retreated again to the
Appalachian Trail, there to hike off my annoyance and
breathe in the sweet smells of moisture and decaying
leaves. Since childhood, walking in nature had been the
one tonic I could count on; without exception, hours spent
with the sky and trees, rocks and rivers, ravens and
canyons, sand and waves and gulls had healed me. Being
in nature and away from the relentless clatter of human
machines -- those we build, and those we can become --
relieved my stress, restored my sense of balance and
brought clarity regarding what was truly important.
Being in nature brought me home -- to myself, to my
center; to my awareness of my place in this vast and
wondrous universe in which humans are but one of many
bold and beautiful and mysterious threads. "*To the*
spirits," wrote Mayan shaman Martin Prechtel, "*the noise*

of the humans was just about the same size as a mocking-bird's song, or a cricket's chirp; we weren't that big to them." What a gift, to realize one's own smallness on an Earth that nurtures all creatures equally, no matter how far some of us have strayed.

This day of hiking was no different from the many that had gone before: My walk into the woods renewed my spirit, and I returned to write in my journal about a book, a "coincidence" and a dream:

"I've begun reading Romancing the Shadow -- a wonderful book. After writing the last entry (the killing-the-gargoyle dream, in which the two aspects of shadow appeared), I discovered to my amazement that Romancing the Shadow talks about the male and female shadow! That was a concept I'd never heard of, or imagined, until analyzing my dream of a few nights ago. Realizing how my soul has guided me to do shadow work -- and how this new book I'm reading is a part of it -- left me feeling a renewed sense of wonder, and of being loved."

I did not write, although it was another piece of this unfolding miracle, that *Romancing the Shadow* had been published very recently, as if it were one of the universe's many gifts to me upon my homecoming from the quest. I also did not write that *Romancing the Shadow* was a book that would have held absolutely no appeal for me pre-quest. I would have passed it by, not even seeing it, just as I had lived with my shadow for nearly 40 years and never known its name.

I wrote next of a dream I'd had the night after the gargoyle dream. As our guides had suggested, I wrote it in present tense, acknowledging that dreams come from a timeless "place" that knows no past or future:

"I am midway down a flight of steep stairs. There are no backs to the stairs, just gaping windows to the ground below; what's more, they seem to be free-standing,

*connected to nothing, made of plastic, perhaps -- very
unstable, shaking and shifting as I move. I stop,
immobilized by fear, unable to take one step further. I tell
someone I'm going to climb back up to the top (for some
reason, less scary than continuing down, yet scary
nonetheless) and will go down another stairway instead.
The person (or is it the Voice?) says those other steps are
steep, too. And I say yes, but not open in the back, and not
so damned unsteady!"*

10 days later -- 48 days Post-Quest -- I scrawled
this note in the margin by my account of the dream:
"*Does this mean that I got too scared to continue on my
post-quest journey? That I did regress -- turn back, or at
least make an attempt to? That I didn't and perhaps still
don't trust the process that is leading me down into
shadow?*" Down into shadow. Some people associate the
shadow with the "underworld"; not coincidentally, the
solo phase of the vision quest is often referred to as the
"underworld" portion of the soul's journey. To
psychotherapist David Richo, author of *Shadow Dance:
Liberating the Power and Creativity of Your Dark Side*,
there is no ambiguity: "The underworld is, of course, our
inner world." In fact, one has to go deep inside oneself to
find the shadow. One journeys down, down, down -- past
ego, past the things we think are true of ourselves, down
into the reality of what it means to be human. Like the
opening scene of the hawk-turned-statue dream, the
reality of what it means to be human isn't all pretty. But
it is universal. That is, to be human is to have a shadow;
and to be human is to have the capacity to act out the
full range of human emotions -- including all the
"unacceptable" ones -- in the full range of ways. I'd begun
going down, but like so many times before, fear had
stopped me. Whether fear would have the last word,
however, remained to be seen.

Chapter 30

> *"You have to love all parts of yourself. In loving your dark side, you take its power away. Isn't that silly? We're taught all our lives to hate our dark side, yet all you have to do is love it and it loses its power."*
>
> -- Ann M. Adams

*3*9 *days P-Q (Nov. 21).* As I descended deeper into this post-quest quest, *Romancing the Shadow* became my guide; in spite of my too-scared-to-descend-the-stairs dream, the authors' questions continued to nudge me gently down the steps, on the path that soul intended.

"*Yesterday,*" I wrote, "*I was trying to figure out what elements of my personality would likely have been relegated to my shadow as a child -- what elements the adults around me would have found unacceptable, just as the adults in their childhood lives had found theirs unacceptable so many years before. What came to me was my imagination. If I'd made up stories -- and stuck to them! -- the way my partner's 7-year-old grandson so often does, I'd probably have been shamed for 'lying.' Perhaps that's one reason I felt until very recently that I wouldn't know how to begin to write fiction, or even to write creatively!*"

For the first eight years after college, I'd been a journalist. Now, I wrote grants to raise money for non-profit agencies. Writing had always come naturally. But

invariably, the writing I'd done had been non-fiction, and
the style I'd used was the style of a reporter -- objective,
a listing of facts in a logical sequence, speaking for themselves, my own voice scarcely more than a whisper. I'd
been a left-brain writer, my "right brain" creative side,
barely engaged at all. *"Finally, I understand. What a gift!
It's not that I'm unimaginative or uncreative; it's that my
imagination and creativity have been locked away. But
they're still here, inside of me. Which means I can find
them. I can use them."* Wow.

The next day, my remarkable insight about imagination's retreat to shadow less than 24 hours old, I could
have celebrated. Or at the very least, written creatively!
But no. Instead, I found myself teaching a class of under-
graduates about grant writing -- and managing, somehow, to have an anxiety attack in the process.

Grant writing was a topic I knew as well as any
other, a topic that I could talk easily about for hours and
sometimes did. (A topic that was, come to think of it, a
relic of the first half of my life, all those years of "left-
brain" writing.) As for teaching, I'd done it countless
times before, before countless people, most of them
potentially tougher audiences than this one. Nonetheless,
in mid-sentence I became acutely aware of the speed and
shallowness of my breath, felt a spring inside me tighten-
ing as the world, too, coiled tighter, moved faster (the
appearance of students sitting quietly at their desks a
gross deception) and I felt, as I'd felt several times in my
life before, that if I didn't faint first, chances were quite
good that I'd explode. So I excused myself from the
classroom, splashed water on my face, took a drink at the
fountain, and returned to face the class again. And, as
always, I managed to talk my way through until class's
end. But I'd been left feeling shaky -- *"not so much
physically as emotionally,"* I wrote in my journal -- fear

imprinted on my psyche as, a few weeks earlier, it had scrawled its name across my skin.

On the drive home I talked aloud to myself, trying to figure out what exactly had happened. Why had I felt so frightened and so vulnerable? Speeding along at 65 mph, 40 minutes of a 1-hour drive remaining, I paused in my reverie (spinning wheels going nowhere) and noticed a strange noise. The more closely I listened, the louder it seemed to grow. My eyes now glued to the side-view mirror, I searched anxiously for loose pieces of metal or dangerously bulging tires -- nothing. I knew a service station was only a mile or two away, so I gritted my teeth and kept driving. When I did stop, I was hugely relieved to find that the sound had in fact been "nothing" -- a dry leaf, stuck between the driver's-side door and the body of the car, vibrating wildly. "*Where did it come from?*" I wrote later. "*Why then? What was it trying to tell me?*"

"Much ado about nothing," maybe?

"Anxiety attack," after all, is just a fancier way of saying "fear". Fear run amuck, fear-in-your-face, fear with a capital F. Poking around in my shadow was scary; the qualities there, ones I'd been taught to fear. Not only that, Fear itself dwelled in my shadow; though I was consciously aware of some of my fears, I hadn't met them all. And fears that are repressed into shadow are perhaps the messiest kind; they can leak out anywhere, at any time, without warning. What, after all, is an "anxiety attack", if not a toxic spill of fear?

The leaf seemed to be saying that many of the things I feared were like itself -- noisy but inconsequential. Soon, the leaf would crumble away to dust; someday, perhaps, if I kept shining a light in the shadows, the fears that dwelled there might turn to dust too. It was worth fantasizing about, anyway, as I finished the second leg of my now-relaxed drive home.

Chapter 31

> *"Here is a test to find whether your mission on earth is finished: If you're alive, it isn't."*
>
> -- Richard Bach, *Illusions*

*4*8 *days P-Q (Nov. 30).* "*I realize as I read* Romancing the Shadow *that I would benefit from regular 'shadow work' -- from thinking carefully about questions like 'What attributes of mine were banished to the shadow?' I already wrote about one: creativity/imagination. Here are others: expressing strong emotions, especially sadness and anger; being 'wild' and childlike and raucous; being spontaneous.*

"*My intuition, too, seems to have been repressed into shadow, but that's the case with almost everyone in our left-brained, seeing-is-believing, logic-reigns-supreme culture. Thank god the quest helped to awaken my intuition -- and to give me the courage to learn to trust it!*"

It was hindsight, though, not intuition, that told me this: "*Just reread dreams from the past month. Realized that the dream about being too afraid to continue down the flight of stairs may have been a VERY important one. It occurred three days before my anxiety attack.*" Perhaps the fear the stairs dream hinted at was the same fear with which the anxiety attack bashed me over the head! Could I have averted the blow? Maybe . . .

----

50 days P-Q (Dec. 2). "*Yesterday morning, enacted a ceremony in honor of my stairs dream of several weeks ago, to let my subconscious know I WILL continue down the stairs (the path) that I began with the quest.*" The ceremony was a simple one, and it involved, not surprisingly, walking down some stairs. I chose the basement stairs (backless, though definitely not plastic), deliberately leaving the light off so that I'd be descending into darkness. As I walked, I spoke aloud my intention to continue all the way "down". When I got to the bottom, the ceremony was done. The journey for which it was a metaphor, of course, was not.

That night, I had this dream, recorded later in my journal: "*I am taking an exam for a graduate course. I feel well-prepared; am confident I understand the concepts. Bill (my own internal guide? a wise and loving teacher?) is the instructor. I get the test, and as I begin to read it, I realize it's nothing like I expected. The test is very colorful, and many of the questions are clever -- word plays, reminding me of games or 'tricks'. Others are purely -- and obscurely! -- fact-based. I am unable to answer most of the questions; realize I may flunk this test. But I know it's worth only 10-20% of the grade, so the worst that could happen is I'll get a B for the course. Bill's creativity in writing the test amuses me -- in a way, I even admire it. I also think I'll have to learn to prepare differently for his tests.*"

Hmm. . .What message cloaked itself in a dream of tricky tests and "failure?" Perhaps one message was that I was on the right track, after all. True, the me in the dream (a.k.a. my ego?) was tripped up by tricks and hadn't memorized the right facts. But more important than either of these deficits, I did understand the concepts. And I also had the whole situation pretty much in perspective; though I might fail this test, I knew without a doubt that I would pass the course (the real test? life?). Moreover, Bill amused me, reminding me of "Coyote" the trickster, a recurring figure in Native American mythology. Among other things, Coyote keeps us honest, forces us to face -- and, if so blessed, to laugh at -- our own foibles.

Psychotherapist David Richo put it another way in his book, *Shadow Dance*, which I read nearly two years later: *"Archetypes are typical and recurrent themes of human experience that are articulated in images . . . (and) surround the ego in pairs of opposites. Each has two balanced sides, positive and negative. There is a hero and a villain, a father and a mother, a wise kindly guide and a troublesome trickster."* Amazing, yet again. Bill in my dream (and in life, bless him!) was the wise kindly guide and the troublesome trickster. Even more important, shadow work was teaching me that all the conceivable pairs of opposites were in me, too -- albeit some in consciousness, the others in shadow. And since I was still alive, I still had time to learn to prepare differently for whatever tests Bill, or Coyote, or I, or the world had in store for me.

The next day (51 days P-Q, Dec.. 3). "Last night, this dream: I am in my last semester at school. Turns out I have only two classes -- both taught by Bill, and both about flying. At first I smile at my amazing good fortune -- two classes taught by Bill, two classes that should be fun! But then I quickly become anxious, thinking of being in a plane alone, worrying about hitting the wrong switch. I literally imagine dropping something and accidentally hitting the wrong button or pedal as I bend down

to pick it up. *I also imagine a crash landing."* There's
that fear again. And the suffering of anticipation. But
wait! The dream isn't over: *"Then I realize Bill wouldn't
let any of us up in a plane alone until we were ready. He
would be with us."*

As, always, is our wise inner guide. As, always, is
the Voice of Soul. And yes, damn it! As, always, is that
trickster Coyote . . .

----

*52 days P-Q, Dec. 4. "Another affirmation that I'm
on the path my soul intended. Listening to a tape tonight
by Rick Jarow, I learned that the second chakra is associated with Jung's concept of shadow! The second chakra is
the part of my body where I developed hives on the second
day of my solo. I knew those hives were sending me a
message, but I had no idea what. Who would've guessed
that they, too, were urging me to delve into shadow?
Another non-coincidental 'coincidence'; another syn-
chronicity; another miracle. Another example of the universe's supporting my healing-growing-remembering-re-
membering. Thank you. Ah-ho!"*

Chapter 32

*6*2 *days P-Q (Dec. 14).* Bill and Dianne had offered our group a lifeline to help us hold to the reality of the dream: a letter known as the "talking staff." A round-robin letter linking the questers across the hundreds of miles now separating us, it was unlike most other letters in that it focused not on the external goings-on of life, but rather on the substance of the soul. It was my turn to write. Among other things, I wrote of writing:

". . . *Your heartfelt responses to my giveaway poem really touched my heart, and helped me to know that writing is, indeed, part of my path. Paradoxically (yet another one!), I've worked on my book only once since the quest -- but when I did, the writing flowed in a way it hadn't before, in all 2½ years of work on the manuscript. It's clear to me that the quest put me in direct communication with parts of myself that ego and so-called rational mind had obscured before, which promise to make me a better and more creative writer. And I'm promising myself that I will MAKE the time to write, regularly, this winter. . ."*

Earth Dreams

The "giveaway poem" was a poem I'd written as a gift to my fellow questers, read aloud on the last day of the quest and mailed to each a few days later. The book was one I'd been working on at the time of the quest (not this one!) -- a book that sought, in yet another paradox, to bring hope to the world using a left-brained style of writing. No wonder the writing had bogged down! Hope is not the province of the left brain. No matter what the circumstances, the left-brain / rational mind / ego can find a myriad of reasons to be discouraged or sad or downright immobilized, a plethora of dangers, an endless list of things that could go wrong. The parts of myself with which the quest had reconnected me were elements of the gold in my shadow, though I didn't call them that. What I did write about shadow was this:

"I'd always associated the shadow with so-called 'negative' qualities like hatred and anger (and, sure enough, many such qualities reside there!) -- but I understand now that lots of wonderful qualities (e.g., spontaneity, creativity) can also get buried in our shadows. For me, one of the many ways I'm doing shadow work is getting to know and honoring the part of me that's insecure, that fears doing the 'wrong' thing-- a part that's been banished deep into my shadow by my very capable and confident professional persona . . .(NOT to be confused with the persona who tried and failed to tie the knot correctly on the day before we left for the canyons. In that case, it was my capabilities that were buried in the shadow!) Get it? It's fascinating stuff, and very healing."

And so it was. The journey continues . . .

Chapter 33

> *"You are never given a wish without also being given the power to make it true. You may have to work for it, however."*
>
> -- Richard Bach, *Illusions*

*7*7 *days P-Q (Dec. 29).* On a day between Christmas and New Year's, in the midst of a week when most activity stops and the world itself seems to hold its breath, I drove down a familiar road in an unfamiliar state of mind. Instead of allowing my thoughts to scatter to the four directions as they so often did, I focused my attention on something I really wanted -- something I wanted so badly, in fact, that I could feel its absence as a vacant place beneath my ribs. This thing that I wanted so passionately was actually not a thing; and, paradoxically, it was something I wanted to give, not get: a gift to the Earth.

In a general sense, the journey that had led me to discover this yawning yearning hole inside had begun in childhood, when nature consistently nurtured me. At the time, starting an anti-pollution club was the only gift I could think of to give. In a more specific sense, the journey had begun in The Canyon, when the Earth conspired with my Soul to save me. And in the most specific sense of all, it had begun today with a mental inventory of the organizations I supported -- a belated Christmas list of sorts, written as I drove. I planned to make some end-of-the-year donations, and as I mulled them over, scenery flashing by on either side, its passage blurred like time, I was suddenly struck by this clear knowing:

These organizations, worthy as they might be, were actually only intermediaries for the one I really wanted to thank and to support -- the Earth, the one who had held me in her arms as I cried in the canyons.

"What could I possibly give to the Earth?" I wondered, doubting that there was an answer, knowing I already did the obvious things -- recycling, composting, writing advocacy letters, gardening organically, donating to save land and wildlife, boycotting the worst offenders etc. etc. etc. And then my inner monologue suddenly turned dialogue as some higher, wiser, more resourceful part of myself offered me an answer.

As I wrote later in my journal, *"It occurred to me then to write something -- a story? a book? -- something that would speak to people's hearts, to remind them of their connection to the Earth in a very different, more mystical/magical way than I hope to do with my other book. I told my partner about this idea today, and could barely keep from sobbing."*

For me, tears like these had always been a sign of something true, something deep, something real, something to pay attention to; though I'd never used these words before, I realized now that it had been the Voice that cried them.

Chapter 34

> *"The animals are speaking to us, through us, and with us. They are coming to us, not only in our dreams but in our lives."*
>
> -- Linda Hogan, Deena Metzger, Brenda Peterson, eds., *Intimate Nature: The Bond Between Women and Animals*

Later in the same journal entry, I recounted another drive on the same road, but on a different day and in the opposite direction: "*Saturday, driving home on H.V. Road, I approached a curve, and as I did an image came into my mind of an animal, surprised on the road by a speeding car and unable to escape. Immediately I eased my foot off the gas, slowing down slightly. Then, rounding a curve I came upon a tractor -- huge, taking up all of my lane and then some, going at a virtual crawl, a pickup truck hurtling toward me from the opposite direction, no shoulder to speak of. I had to practically slam on the brakes not to crash into the back of the tractor. The road was wet, too -- terrible conditions for braking suddenly. Afterward, I could feel my legs shaking. That slowing around the curve, however slight, may have*

been just enough to save me (!) Wow. A miracle . . ."
     Appropriately enough, with no transition, my
journal entry then returned to the idea of a book to "give"
to the Earth:
     *"I think of the number of times / ways the Earth
has 'saved' me: the calming effect of walking in the
waves, no matter how aggravated I'd felt a moment before
stepping into the water; the way that going to the
Delaware River and, later, the Appalachian Trail (e.g.,
after I quit my first job) brought me peace; how the trip to
the rainforests of Belize helped me get clearer re my path,
spurring us to change the focus of our business; how 'my
tree' in the forest freed my tears; and how the Earth herself conspired with my soul on the quest -- conspired to
move me onto my journey, conspired to bring me Home."*
     Not to mention the vision of an animal that had
come to me on a winding country road, not a moment too
soon, not a moment too late -- its timing, perhaps like
mine though I couldn't have known it, utterly impecca-
ble.

Chapter 35

> *"In the beginning, all you've got is the dream. All*
> *you've got is a feeling that wants to be free. But*
> *how does it happen, how does it come to be?*
> *What is the secret, and where is the key? You've*
> *got the vision, but how do you make a start?*
> *You've got to listen close, and follow your heart."*
>
> -- Jan Garrett, "Make It Real"

5 *days later, 82 days P-Q (Jan. 3).* A spring-like
day, nature thumbing her nose at the calendar humans
keep. I was writing in my journal, about yet another
dream about yet another vision quest, this one, not
unlike the real one, ending not exactly as I'd hoped. In it,
I'd been left wandering, feeling heavy, saddened by the
gap between what I'd expected and what it was I'd found.
But at the last minute, Bill rode by in a covered wagon.
He invited me to climb inside. "*I am pleased,*" I wrote in
my account of the dream. "*He has chosen to reward me*
(for my loyalty? my perseverance?). My life will be easier
-- I'll be protected from the rain."
　　　I immediately saw a connection between the
dream and the way I'd been feeling, yet again -- "down",
caught in inertia, saddened and heavy. Geez, I was

getting tired of feeling this way. *"Connecting with the parts of myself that I 'met' on the quest certainly has not been all joyous,"* I wrote. Remembering the mangy hawk, how could I have expected anything else? *"And what of Bill, my guide, 'rewarding' me for perseverance? Giving me shelter? Perhaps that simply means that I will be rewarded -- that I need to keep moving, slowly as it sometimes seems. . . And so, I'm going up to the computer now to write."*

And I did, for only the second time since the quest. The result was this poem:

Vision Quest.
Its greatest meaning
emerging not from the quest itself,
not in the me who sat alone in The Canyon,
inhaling peace through every pore,
but from the journey that started when the quest "ended".
In the now.
And in the now, I hurt.

Take your vision home and share it with your people,
the wise guide said.
If you don't, you'll miss the point,
risk depression,
insult Great Spirit,
endanger your new-found passion.

But what if I've found that "my people"
are not people?
that they are the four-leggeds, the winged ones and tree beings,
the rocks and streams and sky?
That they are, in fact, the canyons?
And what if the vision
I have to offer is something they don't need
Because it's theirs,
always was.
Because it's they who gave it to me?

And all around me, I see my people dying.
To help them,
I am called to share their vision
with The (2-legged) People,
who may or may not be "mine"
But how?
How to convey a truth far deeper
than the surface on which the ego floats?
far richer
than the coveted bank accounts of the adored, the admired, the
wealthy?
far more freeing
than the buy-this, buy-more, buy-now culture
of the so-called "free" so-called "world"?

How to conquer my own demons?
the demons of hopelessness,
of anger,
of cynicism,
of pain?

How to learn to speak in words
the forgotten language of the forgotten heart?
And how, then, to speak it loudly enough
that somehow,
enough of The People hear
that humankind can once again
gaze into the eyes of a wolf
and see not a target, but themselves?

Is this but a dream?
One can only hope so,
since it is from dreams that the world
is created anew
each day
each moment.
Beginning.
Now.

Chapter 36

"It is hard to follow one great vision in this world of darkness and of many changing shadows. Among those shadows men get lost."

-- Black Elk, as reported by John G. Neihardt

The next day (83 days P-Q, Jan. 4). I awoke, fresh from my dreams, feeling alive in a way that I hadn't since the quest. The gloom I'd felt for days had lifted; in celebration, I took Cedar for a two-mile run under skies blue as a robin's egg, and equally unseasonable. Though more than a month had passed since my last run, I found this one invigorating, our pace brisk, the not-quite-cold air bracing rather than sharp like jagged glass to my nose and throat and lungs. Who could have guessed that the act of writing would be such a powerful antidote to depression? Or, more accurately, perhaps, to the shadow cast by Shadow? Or, perhaps more accurately still, to the unsettled feeling that there was something I was supposed to do with my vision, except that I had little idea what, or how. And a vision unshared, as my poem reminded me, becomes very very heavy. Somehow, the writing of yesterday had made me feel light and free, so running wasn't the only thing that came easily. Still

breathing hard, I walked into the house, headed straight
to the telephone, and called my biggest client. After all
the hints the universe had been giving me, I finally got
the message: The way I was supposed to share my vision
was through writing! And so, I would write, full-time.
Starting now. Listening with only half a mind to the
ringing of the phone, I watched rainbows shimmering on
the wall, cast by light reflected through a clear glass bottle on the windowsill. . .

Wait! That's not how it happened. This, this is
what really happened: I woke up, had breakfast, read the
newspaper (always a mistake, since the paper contained
little more than the darkest shadows of human nature,
glorified), petted the dog, wasted a little time. Then I sat
down at the computer . . . and nothing happened. I
couldn't write. No inspiration came. I felt an oppressive
melancholy that I couldn't shake. I got up, stumbled list-
lessly through the rest of the day. It didn't help that in
two days I'd have to go back to work -- my first consulting job of the new year, a meeting in which I'd have to
act alert and competent and clear. And what an act it
would be. When evening came, I considered calling a
friend from the quest. But it was too early; she was in
Colorado and probably not home from work yet. So I
pulled out my journal, and in the writing realized that
my desire to call my friend was in large part a desire to
get back in touch with the parts of myself my friend had
recognized -- the me who had returned from the canyons,
the 'best' of me. My soul. Where had the best of me
gone?

In my journal, I proceeded to label the "worst" of
me -- the parts of myself that I was ashamed of, the
parts that had long ago been relegated to shadow.
Romancing the Shadow used a metaphor of King Arthur
and the Knights of the Round Table, with the King

representing the whole Self, and each knight representing a character or part of oneself with a much narrower
view than the King's. Each of these "knights" -- you could
call them subpersonalities, I suppose -- has a particular
interest or perspective or fear to protect. In a personality
in which these characters or subpersonalities aren't fully
understood -- as occupants of the shadow typically aren't
-- there is always the potential that one of them will
wrest "control" from the King, causing disharmony and
suffering and, often, behavior that seems out of character
or embarrassing or self-destructive. So, who were the
knights around my shadow table? What parts of myself
dwelled in shadow, occasionally emerging in bursts of
indignation or rage or fear?

"*The judge, for sure. The frightened little girl. The
pouter. The sad one, and the one who is overwhelmed by
the world. Oh, and there's definitely the selfish one, and
the resentful one. And the worrier / 'awfulizer', who can
imagine terrible consequences no matter what the
scenario. And the one who won't let go. And the one who
expects rejection. Wow. A full cast of characters. And I'm
not even sure I've named them all. So -- what do they
have to teach me? How can I honor them so that they
have less control of me? Not sure.*"

My list of characters, daunting as it may seem,
was a clear testament to my mood: It contained only the
"dark" side of shadow, with no hint of the gold. Nowhere
on the list appeared the name of the playful one, or the
creative one, or the spontaneous one, or, for that matter,
the one who could write this book. And having focused
solely on the qualities that seemed to me to be negative,
it's no wonder that I had this dream, three nights later:

----

*86 days P-Q (Jan. 7). "I see a small, 'inanimate'
object in the shape of a figure with a face. As I watch, the*

*figure pokes at another object, pushing it toward me.
Chills run down my spine; this figure should not be able
to move. It is definitely sinister -- malicious -- evil --
possessed by some negative and powerful energy. I have
some sort of rod or stick, and I start to poke or strike at it,
not very hard at first. I contemplate breaking it to pieces,
but then I worry about what would happen to the evil
spirit if I did. Would I release it into the world? Could it
ever be contained again? I feel I need to ask someone the
answers to these questions before I bash it in. (Awoke
afraid.)"*

Did the "inanimate" object represent the dark side
of my own shadow, and the dream, my fears of exposing
it? Or did it represent some external manifestation of
evil -- someone else's shadow, acting out? Did the
distinction really matter? After all, shadow work was
teaching me that there was nothing I could see in someone else that did not also exist in me, at least in the form
of unrealized potential. Even more important, who was
this "someone" I needed to ask for answers, before I
risked loosing the shadow upon the world? I didn't know,
though I suspected perhaps it was me.

Chapter 37

"'So then it is up to us,' said the priest. 'It is our work, and either we will do it, or it will not be done.' "

-- Doug Boyd, *Mad Bear*

*8*8 *days P-Q (Jan. 9)*. My partner and family decided to go out for dinner, an impromptu celebration of the subtly lengthening days of winter. I felt ambivalent about joining them. In the end, the urge to write that had been building slowly, like a seedling gathering momentum to burst from fertile ground into sunlight, won out, more powerful than my desire to relax into a meal that I didn't have to cook or clean up, with people who were sure to make me laugh. I went upstairs, sat down at the computer, and began to write:

"How the Earth Saved my Life. I typed the words and then sat staring at them, wondering what came next . . ."

Chapter 38

> *"Surrounded by so much truth, it's a puzzle how we ever came to deny it."*
>
> -- Margaret Wheatley

*1*05 days P-Q (Jan. 26). A typical Monday in winter -- cold temperatures, light winds, a few clouds, idle longing for the weekend past. In the afternoon, a meeting with a client, also typical -- no particular excitement or challenge or surprise. In the evening, a little TV (Bill's no-television prescription having gone as yet unfilled), it, too, typical -- a few laughs, a lot of wasted time, no food for the soul, no silence in which to hear the Voice. But later, when I lifted my journal from the bedside table and starting writing, the typical was gone:

"*Realization: What happened to me on the hike out of the canyons, so desperately focused on my own 'survival' that I couldn't have cared less about the Anasazi ruins, was a perfect metaphor for human kind -- or human not-so-kind, more accurately. Totally preoccupied with survival and self-interest, I lost the ability to see. The big picture -- the diverse and beautiful and richly alive world around me -- simply vanished. Instead, I was driven by fear and a desperate attempt to control -- to control something, even if it was just one foot in front of the other. My thoughts about the cryptobiotic soil ('Can't*

*you see that I'm barely hanging on? If I have to crush
some goddamn crypto to save myself . . .I'll do it!' In other
words: My life is more important than the life of the
desert) -- those thoughts were a manifestation of my fear
and a resulting narcissism that saw nothing beyond my
own two feet. And that's the problem -- when a human
being feels threatened, whether the threat is 'real' or not,
there's not much else that matters.*

*"AND, what constitutes a 'threat' often depends
almost entirely on the scenarios that play out in one's
mind! In other words, people create their own realities --
they imagine dangers or insults or threats. And then they
do whatever they need to do to protect themselves from
that which they've imagined!" In large letters scrawled
across the bottom of the page, I wrote "FOR THE BOOK,"
arrows pointing to the narrative above, and "Thank
You!!!"*

*"So how can I be so judgmental?" I continued.
"Another ah-ha! More about SHADOW. Dianne (co-guide
on the quest, therapist, 'shadow worker') told us that as a
former anti-war protestor, she'd needed to come to terms
with the part of herself that could kill; I, passionate
defender of the natural world, have to come to terms with
the part of me that could participate in the destruction of
a habitat, the killing of wildlife, the deeper wounding of
the Earth. And if I can come to terms with that part of
me, I'll be able to escape the prison of duality -- the we/
they, 'good guy'/'bad guy' righteousness that in most cases
does nothing but drive deeper wedges between people and
thereby make matters worse. In other words, if I can
approach my work and my activism from a place of love
instead of judgment, I'll have a much better chance of
being effective in advocating for the Earth!"*

As often happens when one listens carefully to the
Voice, the realizations and ideas kept on flowing, just as

they had on the day of the elders' council: "*Virtually any animal will act to defend itself if its life is threatened. Yet only humans, as far as we know, have both the ability and the proclivity to imagine -- and respond to! -- a wealth of subjective 'threats'; it is in defending against these threats of our own creation that the worst peril lies!*

"*For example, so many humans have come to equate material things with life -- or, more accurately, to mistake material things for life -- that any seeming threat to their ability to accumulate more and more and more feels like a threat to their very lives. So it is that the rich man -- or, more likely, the corporation he founded, whose voracious hunger he now struggles in vain to feed -- levels jungles, caring nothing about the indigenous people whose very lives have been destroyed, or the countless species shoved closer to extinction; to him, his growing 'richer' is the way to sustain his life. I can abhor his behavior from now until I die -- and I will. But deep down, that man is afraid; and in acting to 'protect himself', he's not so different from me, stepping on cryptobiotic soil as I stumbled past the canyon's edge, refusing to look down and yet 'seeing' nothing but a steep drop-off and the sharp and unforgiving edge of my own crippling fear.*

"*Wow. Thank you, the Voice! And thanks to Edward Abbey, catalyst!*"

I'd been reading Abbey's *Desert Solitaire*, an impassioned tribute to the Utah wilderness. Abbey's words transported me back to the desert and did the seemingly impossible -- made me love it even more. That love, as all love does, removes blockages, thaws the thickest ice, allows the waters of life to flow free. Understanding flows, too, sometimes in a torrent:

"*Reading Rumi, somehow another catalyst. Opened the book to these words: 'DON'T WAIT ANY LONGER.*

Earth Dreams

DIVE . . . .' Dive into life. Live fully. Share your vision. (Write your book!?)

　　"Realized that my fear of my body -- of illness / imbalance -- holds me back, keeps me trapped. (As long as I could remember, I'd had anxiety about something going wrong with my body. A full-fledged hypochondriac, I wasn't. But frequently fearful, I was. Often, it seemed, I allowed worries about my body to distract me from other things -- from issues I needed to deal with, and from gifts I had to give.) *I will / must / do LOVE my body. Finally, for possibly the first time ever, I did a breast self-exam. I've been afraid to do that -- afraid of finding a lump -- in other words, afraid of my own body! And I understand now that that, too, is a metaphor: my fear of my own body is a metaphor for western culture's fear of the larger body, the Earth! My body sustains me; Earth sustains us all. Yet I've been estranged from my body as most 'modern' humans are estranged from the Earth. Yet more shadow, brought into relief. Fortunately, I can reconnect with my body -- and so can humans, with the Earth!"*

　　And finally, I wrote this: "*As long as large numbers of us deny our shadows, the universe in seeking balance will allow for extremes of darkness. REAL balance must come within.*"

　　In other words: As long as so many humans refuse to see the dark potential in themselves, they project it onto the world around them, thereby inadvertently helping to make the world a darker place. And the universe -- a perfect combination of opposites, paradox manifested in a diversity so rich that the mind can scarcely comprehend it -- constantly seeks equilibrium. When so many people deny their shadows, the equilibrium's disturbed; to restore balance, dark events of frightening power may be made manifest. If all this is true, I thought, then horrific acts of darkness -- violence, cruelty, that which

we call evil -- are in part a responsibility of all of us.
Even all we "good" people who would never deliberately
hurt another but who also refuse to acknowledge the
potential that we could. Wow. Not a welcome thought.

And yet if it's true, this is also true: Each of us has
the ability to change, and so each of us has the ability to
make a difference, the ability to have an effect on what's
happening out there in a world that seems to grow
more frightening by the day. In the words of Carl Jung,
*"Anyone who has found access to his unconscious auto-
matically exercises an influence on his environment."* By
restoring balance within, we contribute to balance without. By acknowledging and loving the shadow within, we
loosen the stranglehold of darkness on the world "without". Now that, that is something I need to hear, I
thought. And that is why I wrote "*Thank you!!!!!,*" with
far more exclamation marks than those represented here.

Chapter 39

> "We live in a dark age, craftily lit with synthetic
> light, so that no one can tell how dark it has
> really gotten. But our exiled spirits can tell."
>
> -- Martin Prechtel, *Secrets of the Talking
> Jaguar: Memoirs from the Living Heart of a
> Mayan Village*

Some days later, on a date not recorded in my
journal, in a moment of near-blinding illumination that
forever removed yet another set of blinders, a thought
burst into my mind. It was a knowing so obvious that
virtually everybody seemed to miss it, as I had until just
now:

Ours is a culture obsessed by shadow!

We are fascinated by the darkness -- but it's the
darkness in others, always in others. That's why the
media have become what they've become -- mirrors of our
unacknowledged darkness, "scandal sheets" and shock
TV bursting with bad news and ugly stories that evoke
fear and rage and righteousness, and sometimes even
applause. Yet paradoxically,

Ours is a culture in denial of shadow!

We deny our personal shadows, unwilling to
acknowledge our own darkness, willing to expend huge

amounts of energy to pretend it isn't there. We deny our cultural shadows, too -- the genocide of Native Americans, the horrific costs to the world of our runaway consumerism, the institutionalization and glorification of violence, to name just three.

If only, I thought, if *only* people would acknowledge their own shadows -- their own potential for darkness, just as I'd had to acknowledge my own potential for 'stepping on' the Earth -- then they wouldn't be constantly projecting their shadows onto everybody else: seeing their shadows in other people, other races, even other species. It could be projection, in fact, that fuels the fear and hatred that some humans feel toward predators -- the wolves, the coyotes, the grizzlies, the big cats. Man himself, after all, is the ultimate predator. But unlike most of his wilder counterparts, man kills far more than he eats; he kills for "sport" and for hate and for "justice" and for convenience and for drugs and for material gain and for no apparent reason and even, in the greatest distortion of all, he kills in the name of God -- and he packs a lot of firepower to do it. That makes man easily the most capricious and most efficient predator of all; and that is frightening. Much more comfortable to focus hatred on four-legged predators than to "own" the predatory shadow of man.

On the subject of projection, Robert Johnson wrote: "*Unless we do conscious work on it, the shadow is almost always projected; that is, it is neatly laid on someone or something else so we do not have to take responsibility for it.*" Psychotherapist David Richo noted that "*In projection we see our own traits in others but not in ourselves. . . As we begin accepting our shadow, we acknowledge our projections of our shadow qualities onto others as truths about ourselves. . . The negative shadow in us is projected onto others as strong dislike or disgust. The positive shadow* (Johnson's "gold") *is projected onto others as admiration or envy."* Carl Jung himself said *"Projection makes the whole world a replica of our own unknown face."*

In other words, we see in others parts of ourselves -- perhaps to try to understand them; perhaps to level on them the harsh judgment that, deep-down, we fear we ourselves deserve; perhaps because our denial partially blinds us; or perhaps because the truth of our own being is too beautiful for us to acknowledge. Which brings up another point: If people explored their own shadows, they'd find the gold, too. Which means they wouldn't have to look outside themselves for heroes; instead, each one of them -- each one of us! -- could become the heroes we've always been, just as the once-mangy hawk grew fully into its strong and beautiful self in the front yard of my dreams.

In a world in which people acknowledged their own shadows, people would be free to see others for who they really are -- a mixture of light and dark, just like themselves. And in being seen for who they truly are, people would be free to be who they truly are -- perfectly imperfect humans, reaching for the light.

Now that, *that* is a quest! That is a vision worth pursuing! Maybe, after all, the holy grail is but a shadow; and the shadow is, if not THE key, then at least A key -- an important yet ever-accessible key -- to the transformation of the world!

Chapter 40

> *"Here comes the bad dream. Here comes the sad*
> *scene. Here comes the boogie man inside."*
>
> -- Jan Garrett, "The Dark Side"

*1*06 days P-Q (Jan. 27). I'd been warned. But the warning had come in the text of Robert Johnson's book, a book I'd read quickly, understanding only a little, hungry for information on shadow but, like a first-time traveler to exotic lands, unable to recognize the fruit hanging from the tree right above my head, ready to nourish me. I'd been gratified when I'd found *Romancing the Shadow* because it spoke in a more familiar language, more comprehensible to my left brain; only later did I dive headlong into Johnson's book again and fill myself up. The warning I hadn't understood was this:

"*Where is the inspiration of yesterday that was so thrilling?*" asked Johnson. He wrote of his own creativity, its expression "*instantly constellat(ing) the worst in me and activat(ing) my shadow.*" In other words, light conjuring shadow. Creative inspiration evoking darkness. A "good day" leading to a "bad." The universe of which we are each a microcosm seeking equilibrium? But having read those words only once and understanding them not at all, I was taken fully by surprise when my mood, buoyed by the day of insights described above, turned dark on this, the very next day. . . taken by surprise as one jumped from behind by a creature previously unimagined and therefore wholly unprotected against.

That night, I dreamed of a large body of water, an island, dead bodies. "*I can't believe no one else can see them or is reacting to them,*" I wrote. The bodies were underneath the island yet visible through a lens of shimmering water, held there by something invisible, unable to float free. Trapped, just as I was trapped by seeing them: "*I am afraid to swim in the water because of the bodies.*" Big, beautiful lake. Three human-scale bodies -- tiny, really, in the context of that great lake. I knew exactly where they were, but still I refused to dive into the water. My fear of the bodies -- harmless enough, their flesh long ago food for fish -- my fear of the bodies kept me from diving in and enjoying the sparkling depths of the lake.

In telling the dream aloud, it seemed obvious that the lake represented my own subconscious and the bodies, parts of myself. Disowned parts of myself, no doubt. Parts of myself in shadow, assuredly. Parts of myself that scared me. Yet there was gold in the shadow, too, as I'd gratefully learned. Would my fear of the bodies keep me from the "gold"? Geez, this shadow stuff was getting old . . . and, come to think of it, quite repetitive.

Chapter 41

4 days later, 127 days P-Q (Feb. 18). "Dream last night: I'm using a computer program to design a cover for a book I'm writing. The one I've got on the manuscript now is dark -- dark green, I think, with a tree on it. I know I want a more attractive, lighter cover. This one isn't compelling or exciting. "William (the dark figure from my past) *is writing a book, too; it's in the final stages. He gets a call from his publisher about the cover for his book. I marvel at the irony: He and I finishing books at the same time! He asks me how I am and I say ' fine. I don't trust you for shit! But that doesn't mean you don't amuse me sometimes.' I feel no animosity toward him."* Wow! Shadow -- its darkest parts, no less -- writing a book. And my feeling no animosity. Imagine that.

Later, I added this to the day's journal entry: *"9:30 p.m. More shadow work today (inadvertent, but shadow work nonetheless). My partner pointed out, quite accurately, that I often focus on the down-side of a situation -- on the negative, not the positive. In other words, the opposite*

137

of how I'd like to view the world; the opposite of how I'd like to be in the world; the opposite of the way I've preferred to see myself.

"Also, I noted numerous times today how incredibly hard on myself I am -- how quick I am to focus on the down-side of me, too! In fact, how I tend to demand the impossible from myself: perfection. Realized one reason I sometimes wish I weren't teaching the Thursday night class (a graduate class I'd never taught before) *is that I feel I need to be 'perfect.' I'm afraid of standing in front of the class and not having all the answers, and I'm afraid of standing in front of the class and having an anxiety attack. Crazy. I've stood in front of thousands of people, on hundreds of occasions. And typically, I'm effective and comfortable. I could count on one hand (two fingers, in fact) the number of times I've felt so anxious that I had to leave the room. Yet I focus on that possibility -- hold tightly to it with my fear. What about loving instead of fearing? What about loosening my grip? Loving myself and my students? As I write, I realize it's yet another example of focusing on the negative. It occurs to me to try consciously focusing on the positives -- my capacities, how much I enjoy teaching etc. And if an anxiety attack comes again, I'll deal with it! But why hurt / torment myself by anticipating one? It's self-punitive -- and I don't deserve to be punished! I deserve to love myself -- to be gentle with myself."*

Classic shadow work: Bringing unconscious behaviors into consciousness; being honest with myself about myself. Nothing flashy or dramatic; nothing that cost money; nothing that required special training. Just openness, which allowed me to really hear what my partner was saying, without becoming too defensive; and honesty, which allowed me to see my own behavior and thought patterns clearly; and self-love, which allowed me to look into my shadow without judgment, and then to envision a better way. But could I live it?

The next day, 128 days post-quest (Feb. 19). Yes, I could. On this day, I was gentle with myself and unusually focused. The prior day's shadow work had been important but fairly simple; it required seeing clearly, and being honest with myself about what I saw: my tendency to focus on the negative; the unrealistic expectations I had of myself; the possibility that I harbored a long-denied belief that unless I was perfect, life would punish me. Today, my shadow work moved figuratively from the classroom to the lab; the task became not knowing differently, but being different, based on what I knew. And my figurative lab was a literal classroom, site of the aforementioned Thursday evening graduate class. Stated differently: Yesterday, I'd looked deep into my shadow; today, I wrestled with what I'd found there. I "wrestled" by standing still. And I won.

"Something inside me has shifted! I stayed conscious today of the fact that love and fear can't share the same space. Once or twice, in front of the class, I felt the first twinges of anxiety. Immediately focused on love -- love for me, love for my students. It worked like the magic love is.(!) Thank you!"

Chapter 42

"There are two ways to live your life. One is as though nothing is a miracle; the other is as though everything is a miracle."

-- Albert Einstein

*1*44 days P-Q (March 7). A rainy Saturday. Driving toward town, thinking about my book and about my rage at the bulldozing of the Earth, the latter a powder keg set off, this time, by yet another "lot for sale" sign standing in front of woods, yet another newly gouged road ripping a farmer's field in two. They co-existed inside me, my book and my rage, and their awkward dance made my movements thick and clumsy. In truth, 25 or so rough pages notwithstanding, my book was not yet a book. It was a story given me to share -- on the surface, a story of shadow, but beneath the surface, a story of light and love and hope and beauty. It was to be my gift to the Earth -- Earth, the ultimate nurturer; Earth, whose living loving presence had introduced me to the depths of my own shadow, whispering the intoxicating promise of my someday being whole. This gift I would offer in gratitude and hope -- hope that humans everywhere would begin to shine loving light into their own dark places, and in doing so become whole. Becoming whole, I knew, meant seeing the "whole-ness" not just in oneself but also in the beautifully, intri-cately, amazingly interconnected universe of which we are a part. And so, becoming whole would mean awaken-ing from the western world's collective nightmare of sep-aration and domination that threatened to extinguish not just hope, but all of life on Earth.

My rage, on the other hand, burned me. It made me feel hopeless, for the rampant development I saw all around me was but one symptom of a culture out-of-touch with its soul, a culture that substituted "stuff" for substance, filling people up with garbage and leaving them emptier than before. And it was a symptom of a culture that often looked the other way while a few people with a lot of "power" and money did whatever they wanted, whatever the cost. Sometimes, it even praised them! But I knew, too, that there were others who loved the land as much as I, others who honored the spirits of all creatures, even those standing still and tall, their leaves stirred gently by the wind. I knew there were others who understood that the salvation of human beings lay not in the structures built by man, but in the wild places fired by Spirit. And I knew that many people -- most people, perhaps? -- were less supportive of the status quo than they were tired out by it. But how many people would it take to stop the destruction? The thing about my righteousness and my rage -- the thing that nearly crippled me -- was that they made me doubt people. And so, they made me doubt myself, and doubt even more my ability to write anything that would really matter.

A long time later, I realized that that, too, was par-adox -- harboring within myself both hope and hopeless-ness; love and hatred; despair and passion. It was also being human. In *Owning Your Own Shadow*, Robert

Johnson wrote of "the miracle of paradox":

> *"To transfer our energy from opposition to paradox is a very large leap in evolution. To engage in opposition is to be ground to bits by the insolubility of life's problems and events. Most people spend their life energy supporting this warfare within themselves . . . (But) to transform opposition into paradox is to allow both sides of an issue, both pairs of opposites, to exist in equal dignity and worth. . . If I can stay with my conflicting impulses long enough, the two opposing forces will teach each other something and produce an insight that serves them both. This is not compromise but a depth of understanding that puts my life in perspective and allows me to know with certainty what I should do."*

Johnson's "miracle of paradox" was also a miracle of shadow work -- acknowledging the opposites in oneself and integrating them. But though I'd read his words and been intrigued by the concept of making peace with the opposites, on the day of my drive through the rain I was still, by and large, grinding myself to bits.

And so, unable to clearly hear the Voice, I imagined what the Voice might say. And what I imagined was this:

> *"Don't give up on people. Trust in their -- and your -- ability to hear. Everyone, deep down, is connected to the Earth and to other living beings; the challenge is to reawaken what's already there, albeit buried. Everyone, deep down, yearns for a closer connection with Spirit. And yes, everyone has a shadow; and everyone, deep down, has more than enough light to illuminate it. Even you."* That meant me.

And, I might have added, everyone has the ability to discover and manifest his or her own life purpose. All that's required is to listen, to believe, and to let oneself unfold.

Later, I lay on my bed, mind wandering while my soul listened gratefully to the haunting, heartbreakingly beautiful music of Robbie Robertson and the Red Road Ensemble. And this time, I did hear the Voice. Two phrases were suddenly in my mind, "appearing" from nowhere, behaving as if they'd always been there, just waiting -- for weeks, for months, for years -- for me to turn toward them, waiting for me to hear:

> *Become my Voice.*
> *Carry my Voice to your people.*

I began to sob.

And after I'd had a long and heartfelt grateful cry, I got up and walked over to my computer, sat down and began to write, to give Voice to the story that the Voice itself had 'written':

"*. . . I pour out the iodized water (taking care to aim far from that crystal-clear puddle) and prepare to pump again. This time, the tube will NOT pop out. I'll make sure of it, even though the afternoon sun has begun to tire me, and the hike back to my campsite will surely take longer than did the hike in.*

"*Just as writing the story of the Voice is taking longer. Longer than what? I ask myself, back on the East coast again, facing my computer's glare head-on. Longer than I might have hoped? Longer than I might unreasonably have expected? Longer than the quest itself? Yes and no, to that one. Longer than 11 days, to be sure. But longer than the rest of my life? Hopefully not. Besides, the Voice hasn't finished talking yet, so how could I be finished writing?. . .*"

(definitely not) The End

Post-script

> *"When an inner situation is not made conscious,*
> *it appears outside as fate."*
> -- Carl Jung
>
> *"And if the great fear had not come upon me, as*
> *it did, and forced me to do my duty, I might have*
> *been less good to the people than some man who*
> *had never dreamed at all, even with the memory*
> *of so great a vision in me. But the fear came, and*
> *if I had not obeyed it, I am sure it would have*
> *killed me in a little while."*
> -- Black Elk, as reported by John G. Neihardt in
> the book *Black Elk Speaks*

The following summer, a police officer was murdered in the small town of Cortez, Colo.; the men responsible fled into the redrock canyon maze near Bluff, Utah, where they successfully eluded a search by hundreds of law enforcement officers. More than a thousand miles away, I could feel the peace of the canyons shatter. Something in me shattered, too, as I struggled to understand the metaphor, if any, in this. A large part of my quest was facing Fear. Of all the specific fears that had stalked me prior to my quest, the worst had been my fear of encountering a violent and dangerous man in the wilderness. That particular fear disappeared as soon as I experienced the remoteness and safety of the canyons. But now I realized that the canyons weren't remote enough. And for anyone camping there now -- at the right place, perhaps, but the wrong time -- the canyons were far from safe. What message was I supposed to get? That safety of any kind is just an illusion? That no matter how far one travels, it's never far enough? That my worst nightmare could in fact come true?

That August, I received an unsolicited letter from the editor of a national magazine, inviting me to submit an article for possible publication. At the time, I was about halfway through the first draft of this manuscript. Following is an excerpt from my second "Talking Staff" letter:

"Something that the magazine offer forced me to do -- perhaps the most important thing of all -- was face my fear. I had been writing fairly regularly prior to getting the letter; in fact, the day before it came, I'd thought once again about trying to make my writing the center of my work, rather than continue squeezing it in around the work I do to pay the bills. The letter came, I felt so blessed and excited . . . and for the next two months, I didn't write. I told myself I was really busy with the business (and I was), and with the garden (and I was), and with (blah blah blah -- you fill in the blank). And I started feeling less balanced, less up, less connected to my soul and to my source.

"Finally, something pretty amazing and scary happened, which essentially involved my fears manifesting on the physical plane where I would have to finally acknowledge and face them. . . "

What happened was this: I woke up at 3 a.m. one moonless starless night, startled out of a state of bleary half-wakefulness by the realization that I was hearing something I shouldn't be. It was a strange sound, best characterized by what it wasn't: It wasn't a familiar night-noise, it wasn't the sound of crickets, it wasn't the creaking of the house, and, as I found out a moment later when I stumbled out of bed to investigate, it wasn't the dog licking or scratching or making peculiar noises in her dreams. The sound -- akin to water dripping from a bush -- was coming from outside. And as I leaned toward the window to listen more closely, it shifted to a rhythmic pattern. In other words, the sound was manmade. Someone was out there! I must have gasped -- made some noise, at least -- because immediately the strange sounds stopped. In the eerie silence that followed I heard two distinct footfalls on the loose stones and gravel right outside the house. Needless to say, my fear went wild. I called the police, called the neighbors, began hatching obsessive plans for security lighting, slept poorly for the next few nights. Despite the fact that neither the police nor a friend who conducted a painstaking examination of the area outside the window found signs of a would-be intruder -- despite the fact that my usually vigilant watchdog had slept peacefully through the whole strange night -- I remained afraid. And then suddenly -- miraculously -- something inside me shifted and I began seeing the situation differently.

For example, I saw with sudden clarity that the events of that night made absolutely no sense in a conventional way. After all, the dining room windows below my bedroom had been open; if an intruder had wanted to get in, he could have done so relatively easily. No need to stand outside all that time making odd noises. And then, of course, there were the noises themselves. What was THAT all about? It was crazy; in fact, it was the craziness of it all that was probably the most frightening. And in that sense the whole scenario seemed tailor-made to grab my attention like a bucket of cold water thrown in my face; as long as I could remember, my most frightening nightmares were not of being chased or overtly threatened but rather of "craziness" -- inanimate objects that moved, voices (not The Voice!) that came from nowhere. And now, the sound of water being rhythmically brushed from a forsythia bush?

As I wrote in the Talking Staff letter: "*I remembered that my energy had been really disturbed that night before going to sleep -- I'd been dealing with old, traumatic stuff. And, I had recently experienced a glaring example of my internal emotional state being manifested externally: I'd been in a dark, angry mood, leaving the house to drive somewhere I resented having to go. Just as I began to pull out of the driveway, I had to slam on the brakes to avoid a crazy-looking guy driving wildly, his truck towing a trailer that swung dangerously back and forth across the center line -- a menacing-looking man who glanced my way and leered. Then, less than two miles away on a road I drive often, I passed a pickup truck parked by the side of the road. On its bumper was the Nazi swastika! I couldn't believe what I was seeing; it was hate, displayed proudly, the darkest side of the human shadow glorified. I was so shaken that I mentally stopped short. For whatever reasons -- simple or complex, cause-and-effect or 'coincidence' -- my ugly internal state had been mirrored back to me two times in just under five minutes. I wasn't about to risk a third. And so I changed my mind. I decided to bring to consciousness and then to alter the angry patterns of my thinking -- to do as Jung had suggested -- to effect a change in the environment by making the unconscious conscious. Sure enough, the rest of my drive was blessedly 'uneventful.'*

"*When I remembered that day, and thought of the strange night noises in the context of a world that mirrors back to us our moods and shadows, my feelings began to shift from fear, to understanding and excitement, and then to gratitude. After all, if everything is energy, it makes total sense that what you're experiencing 'inside' can directly affect what's happening 'outside'. In other words, it's quite possible that the noises were caused not by a shadowy intruder but by Shadow itself -- by my own fears, rising from the "grave" of shadow where I'd unsuccessfully tried to bury them!*

"And so I came to realize that that incident had been a pure manifestation of my fear -- fear that had been in shadow; fear that I wasn't acknowledging; fear that, by denying, I'd allowed to take control."

In other words, my fear denied had paralyzed me, which is why I hadn't written for two months. I'm not sure whether I was afraid of getting what I wanted and realizing my dream, afraid of success or afraid of failure. It doesn't matter; what does matter is that I'd pretended I wasn't afraid, and yet I'd let my fear control me. The crazy night noises turned out to be a gift, because they forced me to look at my fear. And when I faced my fear, I got my life back.

"Since all the realizations brought on by that experience," I wrote in the Talking Staff letter, *"I've begun writing again -- and am in the process of simplifying my life to allow for a greater focus on my writing, which is, I believe, my true work, my soul work; and, not surprisingly, doing it makes me happy!*

"And finally, a gift in the writing of this letter: I realized how my book will end -- with that 'crazy' night, a night that occurred almost a year to the day after we left the canyons, and how it allowed me to face my fear, thereby to write! And, believe it or not, I'd had no intention of telling that story when I began to write this letter. It seemed too complicated, and I was probably a little afraid of your reactions (Would any of you think I was crazy?) . . . I am so grateful that this time, I didn't allow fear to stop me. . . "

And the next time, and the next.

What was I supposed to learn from the manhunt in Utah? Perhaps the same thing I learned one Pennsylvania night -- that to be human is to sometimes be afraid. It's true: No matter how far one travels, it's never far enough to escape what it means to be human. It's also true that our worst fears live inside. But they don't have to stop us from living fully, from manifesting our dreams. True courage, someone said, is not in banishing fear but in moving forward in spite of it. Fear puts formidable stumbling blocks in our path. But in the long run, as long as we keep shining light into the shadow -- not with security lighting, but with the light of love -- fear hasn't got a prayer.

An afterword about shadow work

> " . . . the wildest places of all are deep within and
> there's no end to the exploration and enjoyment
> of their mysteries and magic"
>
> -- David Yeadon

November, 2001
   In the three years subsequent to the events
described in this book, I've continued to delve deeper into
the practice of shadow work. In so doing, I've learned
that one of the fundamental questions that puzzled me in
the beginning -- "how DO I love / honor my shadow, without giving it any power?" -- is based on a false premise.
The truth is that shining the light of conscious awareness on a dark element of the shadow automatically
reduces its hold on us. It is in the darkness of denial --
not in the light, and certainly not in the brightest light of
all, love -- that shadow elements enjoy their greatest
power to influence our behavior, sabotage our
relationships and limit the fulfillment of our dreams.
Conversely, bringing loving attention to the parts of ourselves that have been shamed into shadow allows us not
only to reduce the number of times we "act out" in ways
that puzzle and embarrass us, but also to reclaim our full
humanity; work consciously with cruder parts of
ourselves, often polishing them into gems as when

aggressiveness is tempered to assertiveness; grow in self-awareness; reclaim some of our most precious "gold"; develop compassion for ourselves and others; and, ultimately, integrate all parts of ourselves, and in doing so become whole. The closer we can get to a state of wholeness, the more joyous our lives and the better able we are to recognize and to manifest our unique gifts in a world that is starved for our vision and passion and purpose.

Friends curious about the concept of shadow work have asked me about the practice itself -- especially, how to uncover the characteristics hidden in their own shadows. Since I began this manuscript, several excellent guidebooks to shadow work have been published, joining the ranks of those already mentioned. These are listed under Resources. Meanwhile, I encourage anyone interested in shadow work to cultivate the "witness" -- that part inside each one of us that is capable of noticing, more or less objectively, our own thoughts, feelings, actions and reactions. Be especially watchful for intense emotional reactions to the behaviors of others; these are often clues to characteristics that have been shamed into shadow. True, there are some human behaviors so heinous that they would evoke a strong reaction in almost anyone; being sickened by the murderous insanity of a Hitler, for example, does not mean that one is a murderer (although the potential for murder, albeit a dim and distant one, exists inside us all). On the other hand, feeling your "buttons pushed" in everyday situations often points to elements in shadow.

In my own shadow work, I have come to trust that I will not be shown too much at once; understanding comes at a pace that I and my ego can manage. Hence, more than two years passed before I understood that my strongly negative reaction to what I considered narcissistic behavior by a fellow quester was a clue to an element of my own shadow -- a tendency in some circumstances to focus so intently on my own needs and desires that I ignored the needs and desires of others. Now that I've come to recognize it, I have the option of consciously choosing a different way; at the least, I see my own narcissistic thoughts and feelings for what they are -- vestiges of an old pattern that doesn't serve me -- and take care not to act on them. I try never to judge or shame myself; instead, I strive always to love this "unlikable" part of me.

"In this sacred space, I seemed to be releasing a shadow greater than my own, but perhaps one I had tried too long to carry."-- David Richo

----

Just as we see our "negative" shadow mirrored back to us, so we often project our "positive" shadow onto others. One of the clearest examples of positive and negative projection in my own life -- and of the difference between the personal and the collective shadow -- revealed itself to me nearly two years after the quest, shortly after one of several visits to American Indian reservations. As noted earlier, I'd been drawn for many years toward Native American culture and spirituality. And as my lament in The Canyon demonstrated, I'd accumulated an oppressively heavy burden of shame at the genocide perpetrated by my European forebears. The realization that came to me months later, seemingly out of nowhere yet related directly to my continuing shadow work, was that I had projected not only my light but also the light of human*kind* onto Native Americans; similarly, I'd projected all of the darkness onto whites. The truth of the matter lies somewhere in between; cultures are enlivened by people, and people -- all people -- encompass both dark and light.

This is not to deny that some cultures manifest more or less light than others; unquestionably, they do. Rather, it is to say that projecting all light or all darkness onto any one person or race or culture is to do a disservice both to ourselves and to the object of our projection; whether "positive" or "negative", projection is still a trap. Conversely, one of the greatest gifts we can give is to see oneself or another clearly, not through the foggy lens of projection. I have given myself the gift of rediscovering and being warmed by the light in my own culture, while still acknowledging the shadow.

I have given myself another gift, as well -- not surprisingly, the gift of lightness. In projecting virtually all the darkness of humans onto whites and western culture, I'd allowed a hefty share to ricochet onto me. Since then, I'd been "carrying" the collective shadow of western culture; it was a shadow, and a shame, way too heavy for me. Today, I see the dark legacy of colonialism -- a part of the cultural or collective shadow -- no less clearly, but I also see the difference between the cultural shadow and the personal one. I am not personally responsible for the former, though I do whatever I can to shine a light on it. I am not powerful enough to transform the collective shadow, though in transforming my own, I do my part. And in putting the cultural shadow back where it belongs, I have freed myself to interact with all people from a position of balance and self-love, not deficit or shame.

"Darkness cannot drive out darkness: only light can do that. Hate cannot drive out hate: only love can do that." -- Martin Luther King, Jr.

Today, eight weeks after September 11, we are all

living with the ramifications of a harrowing descent into Shadow. In the process, many of us have come face to face with the terrorists living in our own hearts -- among them, hatred and fear so big that it threatens to cripple us. In the language of shadow work, then, one of our challenges is to shine light into our own darkest places -- to transform these inner terrorists, with love -- while shining light into the world's. Another is to combat the particular form of evil that is terrorism without loosing yet more darkness into the world -- including, perhaps especially, in ourselves.

The world has been changed by the events of Sept. 11. Nothing will be the same again; what it will be instead remains to be seen. I do know one thing, however, and that is that each of us has a role to play in determining the face and the heart of this new world.

Which brings me to a final word about fulfilling one's purpose. If I were to say that every day has been bliss and that fear has been but a shadow since my decision to write this book and otherwise manifest my soul's purpose in the world, I'd be lying. In fact, I've learned that the point of facing fear isn't so much to dispel it -- though, happily, some fears do fade away in the enlightenment of conscious loving awareness -- but rather to move forward in spite of it.

What I can say, without a moment's hesitation, is that my life grows infinitely more meaningful and joyous as I seek to better understand and then to manifest my real work in the world. Every one of us came to this Earth with unique gifts to share. My greatest wish for each of you is that you learn to recognize and share your gifts, that you discover and manifest your true purpose. The Earth and all her creatures will thank you. Looking back on your life years later, so will you.

*"**D**eep in our bones resides an ancient, singing couple who just won't give up making their beautiful, wild noise. The world won't end if we can find them."*

-- Martin Prechtel

*"**S**omething beautiful lives inside us. You will see. Just believe it. You will see."*

-- Linda Hogan

Resources

Books on the shadow and shadow work:
Ford, Debbie. *The Dark Side of the Light Chasers: Reclaiming Your Power, Creativity, Brilliance, and Dreams.* New York: Riverhead Books, 1998.
Johnson, Robert A. *Owning Your Own Shadow: Understanding the Dark Side of the Psyche.* New York: HarperSanFrancisco, 1991.
Richo, David. *Shadow Dance: Liberating the Power & Creativity of Your Dark Side.* Boston: Shambhala Publications, 1999.
Zweig, Connie and Wolf, Steve. *Romancing the Shadow: Illuminating the Dark Side of the Soul.* New York: Ballantine Books, 1997.

Other books:
Abbey, Edward. *Desert Solitaire: A Season in the Wilderness.* New York: Ballantine Books, 1968.
Brown, Tom. *The Vision.* New York: Berkley Books, 1988.
Foster, Steven with Little, Meredith. *The Book of the Vision Quest: Personal Transformation in the Wilderness.* New York: Prentice Hall, 1988.
Hogan, Linda. *Solar Storms.* New York: Scribner, 1995.
----------. *Power.* W.W. Norton & Co., 1998.
Neihardt, John G. *Black Elk Speaks.* Lincoln: University of Nebraska Press, 1932.
Williams, Terry Tempest. *Refuge: An Unnatural History of Family and Place.* New York: Vantage Books, 1991.
----------. *Red: Passion and Patience in the Desert.* Pantheon Books, 2001.

<u>Vision quest providers*</u>:
Animas Valley Institute, 54 Ute Pass Trail, Durango, Colo., 81301. Bill Plotkin, Ph.D., founding director. 1-800-451-6327. www.animas.org.
Earthing Spirit, c/o Dorothy Mason, 18 Summerwood Rd., West Simsbury, CT 06092. Dorothy Mason, M.A., L.P.C., and Dianne Timberlake, M.A., M.F.T., guides. (860) 930-8761. Quests for women.
The School of Lost Borders, P.O. Box 55, Big Pine, CA 93513. Steven Foster, Ph.D. and Meredith Little, co-founders. www.schooloflostborders.com.
Vision Arrow, P.O. Box 148, Thompson, PA 18465. Trebbe Johnson, director. (570) 727-4272. www.visionarrow.com.
*For information on quests led by the author, contact Red Road Enterprises, P.O. Box 71, New Tripoli, PA 18066. www.RedRoadEnterprises.org. Other guides can be located through the website of the Wilderness Guides Council, www.wildernessguidescouncil.org.

<u>Organizations working to save wild Utah:</u>
Southern Utah Wilderness Alliance, 1471 South 1100 East, Salt Lake City, UT 84105. (801) 486-3161. www.suwa.org
Utah Wilderness Coalition, P.O. Box 520974, Salt Lake City, UT, 84152. (801) 486-2872. email wildutah@xmission.com. www.uwcoalition.org

<u>Other organizations working for a better world & a healthier environment*</u>:
Alaska Wilderness League, 122 C St. NW, Suite 240, Washington, DC 20001. (202) 544-5205. www.alaskawild.org
Bioneers / Collective Heritage Institute, 901 W. San Mateo Rd., Suite L, Santa Fe, NM 87505.

1-877-BIONEER. www.bioneers.org

   Co-op America, 1612 K St. NW, Suite 600, Washington, DC 20006. 1-800-58-GREEN, (202) 872-5307. www.coopamerica.org

   Earthjustice, 180 Montgomery St., Suite 1400, San Francisco, CA 94104-4209. (415) 627-6700. www.earthjustice.org

   Grand Canyon Trust, 2601 N. Fort Valley Rd., P.O. Box 1236, Flagstaff, AZ 86002-1236. (928) 774-7488. www.grandcanyontrust.org

   Native Forest Council, P.O. Box 2190, Eugene, OR 97402. (541) 688-2600. www.forestcouncil.org

   Natural Resources Defense Council, 40 W. 20th St., New York, NY 10011. (212) 727-2700. www.nrdc.org

   Sierra Club, 85 Second St., San Francisco, CA 94105. (415) 977-5500. www.sierraclub.org

   * More organizations fit into this category every day. These are a few of my favorites.

For information on programs offered by the author, contact Red Road Enterprises, P.O. Box 71, New Tripoli, PA 18066 www.redroadenterprises.com

Elizabeth Brensinger is a writer,
workshop facilitator, vision quest guide
and consultant. She holds a Master of
Public Health degree and is a former
award-winning journalist. In 1993 Liz co-
founded Red Road Enterprises, which
offers personal- and spiritual-growth
adventures from a home base in eastern
Pennsylvania, as well as consulting
services to non-profit organizations.

Mail-in order form

Please send ___ copies of *Earth Dreams* to the following:

Name: _____

Address: _____

City: _____ State: _____ Zip: _____

Telephone (used only in the case of questions / problems re your order)

_____

Email address (optional) _____

I would also like free information on:
☐ upcoming workshops   ☐ vision quests

Enclosed is:

  book cost ($14/book)   _____

  shipping & handling ($3 for first book;
  $2 for each additional to same address) _____

  sales tax (Pa. residents only -- ,84/book)_____

                                    TOTAL _____

**Please send check or money order payable to Red Road Press,
P.O. Box 71, New Tripoli, PA 18066.**

Or ask for *Earth Dreams* at your favorite bookstore